SHOOT ANNUAL 1984

Joy for Man. United's Bryan Robson as he scores against West Bromwich Albion in a League game at The Hawthorns last season. Unfortunately for him, the Manchester Reds lost 3-1.

£2·75

85037-863-X-   © IPC Magazines Ltd. 1983

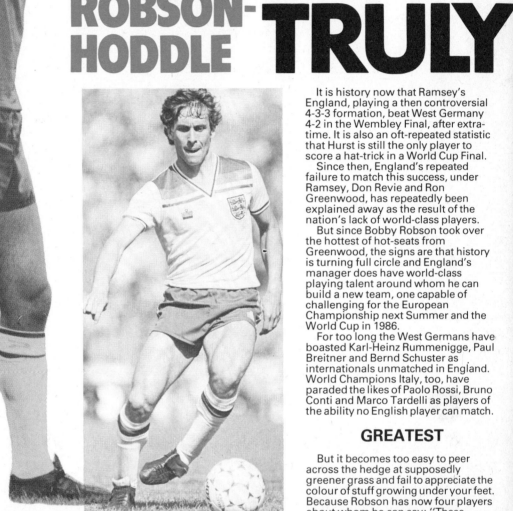

SHILTON-SANSOM-ROBSON-HODDLE TRULY

When Alf Ramsey named his squad for the 1966 World Cup it contained four world-class players: Gordon Banks, Bobby Moore, Bobby Charlton and Jimmy Greaves.

Ramsey knew that with such a quartet at his disposal he could build an England team around them. And when he chose his formation and style of play it led to the shock exclusion of goal-scoring master Greaves whose place went to Geoff Hurst.

It is history now that Ramsey's England, playing a then controversial 4-3-3 formation, beat West Germany 4-2 in the Wembley Final, after extra-time. It is also an oft-repeated statistic that Hurst is still the only player to score a hat-trick in a World Cup Final.

Since then, England's repeated failure to match this success, under Ramsey, Don Revie and Ron Greenwood, has repeatedly been explained away as the result of the nation's lack of world-class players.

But since Bobby Robson took over the hottest of hot-seats from Greenwood, the signs are that history is turning full circle and England's manager does have world-class playing talent around whom he can build a new team, one capable of challenging for the European Championship next Summer and the World Cup in 1986.

For too long the West Germans have boasted Karl-Heinz Rummenigge, Paul Breitner and Bernd Schuster as internationals unmatched in England. World Champions Italy, too, have paraded the likes of Paolo Rossi, Bruno Conti and Marco Tardelli as players of the ability no English player can match.

GREATEST

But it becomes too easy to peer across the hedge at supposedly greener grass and fail to appreciate the colour of stuff growing under your feet. Because Robson has now four players about whom he can say: "These England lads are world-class players."

Peter Shilton is without doubt one of the greatest goalkeepers in the world and possibly of all time. Like his mentor Gordon Banks, Shilton makes the impossible save seem routine and has the confidence and ability to inspire defenders in front of him.

"A truly great player and model professional," says his Southampton manager Lawrie McMenemy. "Peter is worth a fistful of League points to his side every season."

Shilton's form during the last World Cup tells it all. He was beaten only once in five internationals, yet England did not even manage to win fourth place!

This was due to the genuine lack of world-class forwards – the one area

Born Leciester, Peter Shilton is recognised as one of the best goalkeepers in the world. Began with his local club and worked with the great Gordon Banks before succeeding him, both at City and at Stoke. Later joined Nottingham Forest for a reported £270,000 in September, 1977, and won two European Cup winners' medals under Brian Clough. Joined Southampton for £350,000 in August, 1982. Won England Schoolboy, Youth and Under-23 caps before eventually displacing Ray Clemence as England's number one during the 1982 World Cup.

London-born Kenny Sansom began his League career with Crystal Palace for whom he made 172 League appearances before joining Arsenal in an exchange deal involving Clive Allen and Paul Barron in August, 1980. League debut against Tranmere in May, 1975. Won England Schoolboy, Youth and eight Under-21 caps before becoming regular first choice left back for the full England team during the World Cup.

where Robson does have a problem.

Only Trevor Francis of the existing international strike-force comes close to world-class rating. And his inconsistency and repeated unavailability through injury keep him off that level.

But elsewhere Robson can build and feel confident of matching the world's best. Kenny Sansom is now recognised as a left-back of quality, skill and versatility. The Arsenal defender marks tightly and cleanly, can pass a ball as well as any player in the country and has the speed, flair and instinct to break up the line with the

Manchester United's Bryan Robson emerged as a magnificent player during the Spain World Cup. From midfield he scored twice in the opening game against France and has been a regular marksman for club and country over the past three years.

Robson's strength, skill, finishing and vision make him the perfect all-round player. He can play as sweeper, in midfield or behind the front men and excel in every role. He is also a natural leader as proved since he became skipper of club and country.

"Bryan gives you the impression that your squad is bigger than it really

Continental player.

There are those in the game who still say that Hoddle's contribution to a game, especially defensively, leaves much to be desired. Others, however, believe that any period of his incomparable magic is preferable to 90 minutes of sweat and effort by honest but more limited midfield artisans.

Hoddle has what it takes to become England's fourth world-class player. It remains to be seen if Bobby Robson goes one better than Alf Ramsey and builds the winning England team he so desperately wants on all four of his world-class lads.

WORLD CLASS

dash and directness of an orthodox left winger.

"He is a delight to watch and a pleasure to work with," says Arsenal and England coach Don Howe: "because he can operate like two players for you. He has the discipline to know when to support the attack and when to stay tight."

More than that, Sansom can create and score goals because his close control allows him to take men on in tight situations.

Born Chester-le-Street, Bryan Robson, a former England Youth international, won seven Under-21 caps before winning his first full cap, against the Republic of Ireland, in 1980. League debut for West Bromwich Albion against York City in April, 1975 and made nearly 200 League appearances for them before joining Manchester United for a reported £1,500,000 in October, 1981. Scored the fastest goal in the history of World Cup Finals when he put England ahead against France after only 27 seconds in Spain in 1982.

is," says United manager Ron Atkinson. "I rated him so much at West Bromwich that I knew he was a priority signing when I moved to Old Trafford. He seems to get better all the time, even when you become convinced that he has reached his peak!"

Down at Tottenham, the return of Argentinian genius Osvaldo Ardiles proved to be the spark that ignited the slumbering talents of Glenn Hoddle. The Spurs idol threatened to become an international "nearly-man" when, with no fewer than 13 caps after the World Cup he then went off the boil and fell behind in the international stakes. Robson began assembling his new-look England knowing that Hoddle had to wait until January of 1983 before scoring his first goal of the season.

But when Ardiles came back from Paris St. Germain, he picked up where he had left off, providing the ideal midfield partner for Hoddle who quickly snapped back into his exciting shooting and long-passing game.

Here is an England player with the skill and vision equal to that of any

Born Hayes, London, Glenn Hoddle joined Spurs as an apprentice in April, 1974. Youth and 12 times an Under-21 player before breaking into the senior side against Bulgaria in 1979. League debut against Norwich in August, 1975 and rated as one of the most skilful young players in Europe. Specialises in spectacular long-range goals! A member of the 1982 World Cup squad.

FOREST FIRE...

. . . that's what striker Garry Birtles supplies to Nottingham's City Ground club. Garry began with them, and his goalscoring attracted the attention of mighty Manchester United, who paid out a massive £1,250,000 for his services. Unfortunately, he struggled at Old Trafford and his career looked set to plummet, but his old boss, Brian Clough, brought him "back home" for a bargain fee – and Garry's fortunes took off again. Now the fans, and his team-mates, are just wild about Garry!

Paul Mariner has learnt to stop worrying when the goals dry up. "I used to be terrible when I wasn't scoring regularly," he admits. "I'd go home after a barren game, and try to read a book or watch TV. But my mind would be miles away, thinking about my form. Now I'm more positive. I just keep plugging away without getting too worked up. And, sure enough, the goals start flowing again." Paul's always had the goal knack, ever since he drew the scouts to watch him stretching the goalnets at Plymouth Argyle.

The lucky club to land his services was Ipswich Town, who paid £240,000 for him in October 1976 – and he's repaid every penny and more.

Even though he found himself pitted against a higher class of defender in the First Division, he managed to maintain a high scoring rate. Most seasons he's finished top scorer for his club.

He has the greatest respect for the stoppers he faces, as they have for him. "At the end of 90 minutes against the likes of

MARINER MAGIC!

Arsenal's Dave O'Leary and Man. United's Gordon McQueen, I'm completely out of breath."

It was in March, 1977, that Paul had his first game for England, coming on as a substitute against Luxembourg at Wembley. England won 5–0, but he was not amongst the scorers.

In fact, it wasn't until the return game against Luxembourg that he opened his account for England, scoring the second goal in a 2–0 win in October.

It was his goal against Hungary at Wembley that earned England a trip to the World Cup Finals in 1982.

And on the playing fields of Spain he scored in England's first two games – in the 3–1 win over France and the 2–0 win over Czechoslovakia.

He'd like to repeat the experience in the European Championship in 1984 and help England win the competition for the first time ever.

The introduction of three-points for a win has brought about added excitement. And there's nothing more thrilling than the sight of a player scoring the winning goal. Here, Forest's Mark Proctor does just that against Swansea.

THREE-POINT

Dave Johnson has been a scorer of vital goals for Everton in his two periods at Goodison Park. In between he gave valuable service to Ipswich and Liverpool. Here, Dave (left, centre) strikes home the goal that sank Watford last season.

8

WINNERS

(Above) "The Flying Dutchman", Arnold Muhren, fires in Manchester United's three-pointer against Spurs.

(Above, right): Norwich City's John Deehan creates one of the shocks of last season by blasting the goal past Bruce Grobbelaar that beat League leaders Liverpool at Carrow Road. (Right): Aston Villa's Gordon Cowans shows what a cool customer he is by calmly side-footing home the penalty-kick which decided the League game at Villa Park against London's West Ham United.

GARY OWEN
West Bromwich Albion

10

RUSHING TO THE TOP!

The legendary Bill Shankly needed no excuse to talk about the scintillating skills of the thoroughbred Liverpool stars he assembled lovingly in his brilliant Anfield career, or any other great player he happened to admire.

Bob Paisley preferred a different approach when he succeeded "Shanks" as Liverpool boss in July 1974.

To persuade Paisley to wax lyrical about one of his players became as unrewarding as attempting to prise apart two pages of an exercise book

RUSHING TO THE TOP!
Continued from previous page

Ian Rush on his way to getting his fourth goal in Liverpool's overwhelming win over Liverpool's neighbours, Everton.

WARK-RATE

IPSWICH'S GOALGETTING MIDFIELDER IS ALWAYS ON THE GO!

John Wark's remarkable talent for scoring goals from midfield is based on nerve and determination as well as skill.

But then when you consider how Glasgow-born Wark began his career, it will come as no surprise to discover that he possesses his fair share of nerve!

"I certainly chose the hard way of going about things," he said: "because after spending all my early years at Ibrox supporting Rangers I started training with, yes, Celtic! Imagine the reaction of my pals.

"I also thought that I might become a Manchester City player, but after trials and promising moves they took a bit of time deciding and Ipswich stepped in with a firm offer of a contract."

Wark's forceful style of play is laced with vision and skill – and that killer instinct in the penalty area.

He was a cornerstone of Town's F.A. Cup Final victory over Arsenal in 1978 and scored twice in their 5-4 UEFA Cup Final aggregate victory over Dutch side AZ 67 Alkmaar in 1981.

A strong candidate for Footballer of the Year on two occasions, Wark prefers the everyday football life to the bright lights. Polite and an excellent ambassador for his club, he will also take time to encourage youngsters making their early mark in the first team.

"I appreciate the importance of helping and being helped," he said: "I have two brothers who are also in the game; Alex went to play for Bell Park in Australia's Victoria First Division and Andy, the youngest, had trials with Ipswich at 17 without being signed but should make his mark back in Scotland very soon."

Wark was signed by and developed by England manager Bobby Robson during his ten years at Portman Road, adapted quickly to working under Robson's successor, Bobby Ferguson.

"To be honest I said at first that while I admired Bobby as a coach I was not too sure about his managerial talents. But he settled in and things carried on fine."

Wark's scoring knack often sees him winning a tackle around his own box then, seconds later, popping up with a late run into the opposition's area to get on the end of a cross or through ball. Such versatility requires tremendous stamina and fitness.

"Yes, I advise all youngsters to work hard at their game . . . and also keep themselves fit at all times. The work you put into football is always repaid."

John Wark (right) battling hard in the first-leg of the 1981 U.E.F.A. Cup Final against Dutch club Alkmaar. Ipswich won 3-0.

Continued from page 11

Paisley, choosing the quiet approach, encouraged his players to speak volumes on his behalf with the brilliance of their performances week in week out.

So it takes something special for Paisley to "open up" on the players who have helped make Liverpool Britain's most outstanding club in the past 20 years.

Ian Rush, Liverpool's Welsh international striker, is such a man.

Quite out of character, Paisley could retain his dignified silence no longer when he thrilled to Rush's goal-scoring rampage in the 1982-83 season.

"Dalglish and Rush are probably the best goal-scoring partnership in Liverpool's history," he blurted as the Anfield club set a storming pace at the top of the First Division.

What, better than Kevin Keegan's partnership with John Toshack? Better than the Ian St. John-Roger Hunt combination? Better than Billy Liddell's dynamic goalscoring exploits in harness with Albert Stubbins?

"Better than them," repeated Paisley.

Paisley's comments were the final encouragement Ian Rush needed to appreciate that today he is one of the First Division's most exciting strikers.

Centre-halves say his predatory talents in the penalty box make him the First Division's most lethal marksman, more dangerous even than the player they have praised for years, Kenny Dalglish.

Paisley is not alone in believing Rush has become the deadliest striker in the game.

England manager Bobby Robson says: "Ian has proved he is developing into one of the best goalscorers in the country.

"He has speed off the mark and composure in front of goal when having to play in areas where there is little time or space because of tight marking. He is a match-winner."

'BRILLIANT'

Mike England, who blooded him in the famous red shirt of Wales, says: "Ian is absolutely brilliant with his electrifying pace. He is one of the most exciting forwards around."

"One of a rare breed of footballers who can score goals" – that the verdict of Joe Mercer, soccer's elder statesman, who has played against Dixie Dean, Hughie Gallagher and other goal-scoring greats of soccer history.

Rush's priority in 1984 is to establish himself at world level. His overriding ambition is to lead the Welsh Dragons into battle in the 1986 World Cup Finals.

He could be forgiven for swanking about his success already. Thirty goals for Liverpool in the 1981-82 season, well before he had blown out the candles on his 21st birthday cake, earmark the razor-sharp striker for an outstanding career.

His partnership with the rejuvenated Kenny Dalglish in 1982-83 became almost as famous as Butch Cassidy's with the Sundance Kid.

Rush remains unmoved by the success.

Shy and modest, he says: "The main thing is that the team keep winning and that I maintain my place in the Liverpool side. If I do that I must be doing something right."

The Liverpool manager would heartily agree with that sentiment from a player with the right pedigree to go all the way to the top.

Much as Ian is proud of his 1983 League Championship medals, the honour he cherishes most is the Young Player of the Year award.

Voted for by his fellow professionals, it acknowledges someone of exceptional talent.

If Ian continues at his present rate of progress, it won't be long before he receives the senior award!

GARY MABBUTT

TOTTENHAM HOTSPUR & ENGLAND

Autograph: *Gary Mabbutt*

Height: 5 ft 9 in

Weight: 10 st 9 lbs

Birthday: 23rd August

Birthplace: Southmead Hospital Bristol

Nickname: Mabbsy

First club: Bristol Rovers

Favourite food: Steak

Favourite drink: Diet Pepsi and Perrier water

Favourite other sports: Tennis, Squash.

Gary heads for goal in England's 2-0 defeat.

Most memorable match for (country):

My debut against West Germany

Which person in the world would you most like to meet?

The Royal family and Olivia Newton John

Gary's first visit to Wembley as a professional. Unfortunately Spurs lost the 1982 Charity Shield game 1-0 to Liverpool.

Most memorable match at club level:

Charity Shield game versus Liverpool at Wembley

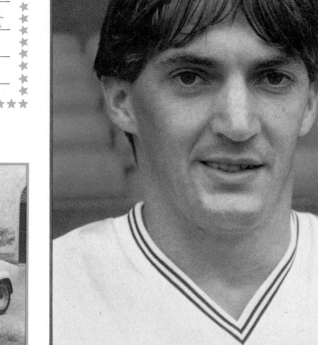

Person who has
helped me most
in my career:

My Father Ray,
John Cartwright
(My England
Youth Manager)

Car I'd like to have:

Lamborghini Countach

Present car:

Ford Sierra 2 litre Ghia

My best friend in football:

My Brother Kevin
at Crystal Palace F.C.

Football hero
of childhood:

Bobby Moore

Favourite TV show:

Minder.

Dallas.

Top of the Pops

Peter Reid is waiting for
The Goodison Park EXPLOSION

Everton midfield star Peter Reid is sitting right on top of a time-bomb – and he can't wait for the explosion.

The former England Under-21 international believes there is so much potential at Goodison Park that it will need only the tiniest spark of success to send the whole place soaring.

"All that Everton have lacked in recent years is confidence and consistency," claims the man signed from Bolton in December, 1982, for a knockdown £60,000.

"If we can achieve consistency, then confidence will follow automatically. It is essential that we go out every week expecting to win.

"As soon as we develop that kind of positive attitude we will really go places."

From a personal view, Reid is revelling in his return to big-time soccer.

OUTSTANDING

During Bolton's two years in the First Division, he had been one of their outstanding players.

Six Under-21 caps gained in 1977 and 1978 further emphasised that his future seemed assured.

But a crippling series of injuries, coming as Bolton slid back down to the Second Division in 1980, combined to thwart Reid's ultimate ambition of gaining a full England cap.

A broken knee-cap first sidelined Reid, rapidly followed by a cartilage operation, damaged medial ligaments and a broken leg.

"Football is a physical game, and knocks are part and parcel of it. I suppose I've been unfortunate with injuries, but I don't really like to harp on about them."

Nevertheless, he cannot completely overlook the large chunk of his career which was devastated by those operations.

"It's very difficult to come back from a major injury. First you have to get fit, and then you have to get fit enough to play top-class professional football – and that's the big problem."

Having taken so many blows, however, Reid has now adopted the outlook of never looking any further ahead than the next game.

"I've still got plenty of ambitions left within the game, but I never take anything for granted any more."

His only aim at present is simply to retain his place in the Everton team.

"There is such a fantastic first team squad here that it is a real battle just to get a game.

"Everything at Goodison Park is geared towards success. Coming to Everton has been a marvellous move for me.

"I was amazed at just how quickly my transfer went through.

"I'd been trying to move from Bolton for quite a while without anything definite developing.

"Then a figure of £60,000 was mentioned in the newspapers and everything suddenly took off from there.

"Sunderland, Luton and Sheffield Wednesday all came in for me, but as soon as I knew Everton were interested there was no choice to make.

"Everton boss Howard Kendall phoned me at home and I agreed to sign there and then – without even discussing personal terms."

Reid, Merseyside born and bred, was delighted to stay in the area. In fact, he could have become an Everton player two years earlier.

Former Goodison boss Gordon Lee agreed a fee of £600,000 with Bolton in 1980, but Reid could not agree terms and rejected the move.

WORST CRITIC

"I'm often asked if I now regret that decision," says Reid. "All I can say on the matter is that that is something which happened in the past, and I would prefer to talk about the present."

But does the fact that when he finally did move it was at just a tenth of Bolton's original asking price bother him?

"Not at all. I have nothing to prove to anyone but myself. I am my own worst critic, you really wouldn't believe just how self-critical I am.

"I want to perform so well that even I will be satisfied with my form. Because if I'm playing that well, *nobody* can have any complaints."

16

BATH LAUGHS

"Wrong timing by the ref – you've got another five minutes to play"

"He always washes his gear at the same time"

"Tell the Manager this is no way to get rid of a bad team"

"Our new £300,000 player is beginning to settle in, I see"

Since I first became involved in the game way back in 1957 I've seen and played with literally thousands of footballers.

Having scored a few goals in my time, one question I'm always asked is which striker I rate as the best to have graced the Football League during those 26 years.

I've avoided answering that question like I avoid the plague. Even now I'd never attempt to pick out one name and say that he was *the* best.

What I will do is to give a list of ten names. These players, in my opinion, best represent British strikers of my time.

There are literally hundreds of great players whose names won't feature in the list. Men of the calibre of Frannie Lee, Jeff Astle, Frank Worthington, Joe Royle, Peter Osgood, Allan Clarke and Joe Jordan are all conspicuous by their absence.

I'd like to apologise to them all now. I'm sorry, lads, I just wish I only had to narrow the field down to a thousand or so.

Even defining the word 'striker' has given me a few headaches.

I believe that a striker is someone whose sole job in the team is to score goals. That's why you won't find Bobby Charlton, Trevor Francis, Mike Channon, Martin Chivers or even Georgie Best in the list.

Bestie was quite possibly the finest footballer I have ever seen. Yet although he scored more than his fair share of goals, there was so much more to his game. That's why I don't classify him as a striker.

Please don't write to me about the names I've missed out. I realise I've walked right through a minefield by even attempting to name my top ten. I should have kept my mouth shut. But it's too late now . . . so here goes.

'My top

Arthur Rowley (left) in his Fulham days. Brian Clough was unfortunate only to gain two caps for England. Here he's in dynamic action in his last game, when England lost 2–3 to Sweden at Wembley in 1959.

'He Took His Time'

ARTHUR ROWLEY. Arthur was just coming to the end of his career as I was starting mine, so he only just qualifies for inclusion. But anybody who scored 433 league goals in an 18-year spell cannot be ignored. Okay, so he took his time, and his goals were scored at all levels of the Football League. But he was what I call a dedicated goalscorer. I liked Arthur's style, because it was my style as well. And it was the style of all truly classic strikers.

'Fantastic Strike Rate'

BRIAN CLOUGH. Fortunately I'm back in my old mate Brian's good books, so nobody can accuse me of trying to butter him up! His career as a player

ten strikers'

has been overshadowed by his career as a manager, but believe me when I tell you he was one hell of a striker. Cloughie scored 251 goals in 274 League games for Middlesbrough and Sunderland – a fantastic strike rate. Most current strikers don't even *play* in 90 per cent of their team's games. He was a fearless player with a terrific shot. He had a tremendous partnership with Alan Peacock at Boro. Cloughie was terribly unlucky to win just two caps for England. I played with him in those games against Wales and Sweden in 1959. The team was then picked by a three-man committee and was probably the worst England team I ever played in. Cloughie and I were both axed after that. I got back in and he didn't. He still has a go at me about it!

'Either Him Or Me'

ROGER HUNT (below). Roger to me was exactly what every great striker should strive to be. He didn't have a great deal of grace or style, but he was always there when you needed him. I suppose he was fortunate to have played alongside Ian St. John at Liverpool. "The Saint" was a terrific player. I'd have loved to have played with him. Yet it was Roger who scored all the goals. You could rely on him to get you 30 goals a season. Roger and I played together for England on a number of occasions, although for quite a while it was either him or me. He was always on hand to help me out when I got myself into trouble. I remember a game against Norway in 1966. We won 6–1 and I was lucky enough to bag four of them. Roger didn't score that day, but his help was invaluable.

19

Continued from page 19

'My Favourite'

DENIS LAW. Without hesitation I would name Denis Law as my favourite footballer of all time. In my eyes, Denis could do no wrong. He was magic. Georgie Best even took a back seat to Denis. He was only a spindly little character, but he more than made up for a lack of physique with his genius. He was athletic, acrobatic, brilliant in the air for such a little lad and so quick. He also had bags of personality to go with it. That's the trouble with today's game. There are no Denis Law's about.

'A lovely feller'

BRYAN ROBSON. I would advise any aspiring young striker to take the trouble to see Pop Robson in action, because this man is the last of a dying breed. He concentrates solely on sticking the ball in the net, and just one look at his record proves how successful he's been at it. Pop goes in where it hurts and although he's lost some of his pace now there used to be no catching him once he started to go for goal. How he never won an England cap remains a mystery to me. We played together when I was winding up my career at West Ham and I think he's a lovely feller. The greatest thing about Pop was his timing. His forward runs were perfectly judged, and he was so quick he could even make one of my terrible passes look great.

Denis Law, then with Manchester United, scores against Everton in the early Seventies.

'Never happy unless he scored'

MALCOLM MACDONALD. Malcolm was brave, strong as a lion and could run like the wind. But his greatest attribute was that he was never happy unless he scored. Malcolm would try a shot from anywhere rather than pass the ball, and I've seen him claim some amazing goals. But that was all he worried about. He could play the greatest game in the world and come off the field at the end of the day absolutely sick because he hadn't put at least one away. He's in the international record books for scoring five goals against Cyprus for England and I can't see any of the current team getting anywhere near that.

'Most exciting'

KENNY DALGLISH (right). I would never like to get involved in an argument as to who is the greatest player ever to wear a Liverpool shirt, but I know for a fact that Kenny Dalglish would come very high in the reckoning. Some people would say he's not a striker by my definition, because he isn't there just to score goals. But he *is*, it's just that he is so good at so much more than just sticking the chances away. Every time I see Kenny in action he's dribbling, turning, shooting and tearing defences apart. He's always looking to do something different, which makes him one of the most exciting players in the game today.

Jimmy played with Bryan Robson at West Ham and regards him as a model goalgetter. Malcolm Macdonald (right in stripes) holds a record unlikely to be beaten.

Liverpool never thought they'd be able to replace Kevin Keegan, but Kenny has proved to be an even better investment.

Ipswich Town's Ray Crawford — one of Britain's finest Post-War centre-forwards.

'Upset Defenders'

BOB LATCHFORD. A big, strong lad who has consistently scored goals for more than ten years. Bob had a lot of critics when he was in the England team a few years ago, but I certainly wasn't one of them. He had a rough ride because he was playing in one of the worst England teams for a long time and they never once played to his great strengths. He's virtually unbeatable in the air and you can rely on him to stick away any chance in the six-yard box. I remember towards the end of my career this strapping great centre-forward playing for Birmingham. He certainly upset more than his fair share of defenders.

'Never left the penalty-area'

RAY CRAWFORD. When Ipswich won the Championship in 1962, Ray had a tremendous partnership with Ted Phillips, who was another prolific goalscorer. But even after he left Portman Road in 1963, Ray continued to score. He was an out and out striker, the kind of player who never left the penalty-area. He put so much pressure on defenders that the rest of his team had a field day. Opponents were so busy looking out for big Ray that they virtually ignored the rest of the team. It saddens me that very few people really remember him, because he was one of British football's finest Post-War strikers. Unfortunately, he'll go down in history simply as the veteran who scored two goals when Colchester beat Leeds in the 1974 F.A. Cup.

Bob Latchford (right) "upset more than his fair share of defenders."

'Silenced his critics'

TED MacDOUGALL (above). Ted scored goals at virtually every level, and he scored a hell of a lot of them. Like nearly all Scotsmen, Ted always felt he had something to prove to us Sassenachs. He had a cynical approach to the game and this helped him tremendously over the years. He believed that scoring goals was the only way to shut up his critics, and he certainly silenced quite a few. To be perfectly honest, I took a long time before including Ted. Ideally, it would have been my top twelve, because then I could have included the names of Kevin Hector and John Richards. But Ted MacDougall it is.

So there you have it — my top ten. Looking over the list even now the names of hundreds of great goalscorers I'd almost forgotten come to mind. Purely in terms of statistics, I suppose I should have included Terry Bly and Dixie McNeil, but in their cases I'll use the excuse of the fact that they didn't do it in the First Division.

As for the future, I'm sure that Liverpool's Ian Rush will one day be added to the names above. Maybe Paul Walsh and even Gary Shaw will also join him. Who knows?

But when you're talking about great goalscorers, it's almost like cricket. You can't really call somebody 'great' until they've proved their worth over a number of years or until their careers are finally over and they've stopped kicking the ball in anger.

I think the best way I can justify my selections is simply by pointing to facts. The ten men I have just named had, at the time of writing, clocked up the grand combined total of 2,558 goals in League football alone.

And that's entertainment in anybody's language!

GARRY'S DEBT TO SWANSEA CITY

side. But it does nothing for your confidence.

"So when John Toshack came in for me I could not turn him down. And I must admit, it was like home from home when I arrived at the Vetch Field because I met ex-Evertonians Neil Robinson and Bob Latchford and ex-Liverpool lads Ray Kennedy and Colin Irwin.

"Now I have played for three League clubs and touched the fringes of success, but I'm still waiting to put one major medal on my empty sideboard. And I reckon I owe it to Swansea to achieve a double ambition — success for me and for them."

Early Chelsea days saw Stanley being compared with Bobby Charlton as his stylish running, eye-catching passing and explosive shooting swept him into the England reckoning. Then injury took its toll, and by the time he'd recovered, a measure of sharpness was missing.

But before that injury Stanley was wowing the terraces. Fans expected things to happen when he received the ball and his stylish play reminded them of an era at Stamford Bridge when the likes of Peter Osgood, Charlie Cooke and Alan Hudson were at their peak.

It was something of a shock when Stanley was allowed to move up to Goodison Park, and he recalls those

Everton days without a great deal of enthusiasm.

"I spent two seasons with Everton and we never looked like winning anything. Yet the whole set-up was geared to success and the players longed to upstage Liverpool. My goals dried up. I scored only one League goal in 52 appearances for them, and while I did play a number of games in defence, that's no excuse.

"I've picked up a few again since moving to Wales and now I desperately want to be part of a Swansea side that picks up a trophy. I owe it to them because the manager, fans and teammates gave me the life I needed when I needed it most.

"John Toshack has worked very hard to get things right at City and has earned the respect of his players. But the novelty of being up in the First Division has worn off after two seasons. Now is the time to make our mark. I certainly want to make mine."

Swansea City gave Garry Stanley a First Division future at a time when his confidence had all but deserted him and the 28-year-old Midlander is determined to repay them on the pitch.

Stanley, once a member of the 1977 Chelsea promotion side that threatened to launch a new era of Kings Road swingers on the First Division, surprised many of his fans by moving to Everton after a long spell out of the side with injury.

It was not a happy two seasons at Goodison Park and ended with Burton-born Stanley beginning to feel that he was unwanted.

"Howard Kendall didn't seem too bothered whether I signed a new contract or not when things came to a head. I decided to sit tight and gave 100 per cent in the Central League reserve

'WRONG MOVE WRECKED MY ENGLAND CHANCES'

The heart-breaking difference between genuine success and failure can be as small as your own signature on a contract, according to Norwich city striker John Deehan.

The Birmingham-born goalscorer is no longer bitter abut his failure to make it to the full England team – but he reckons the disappointment will stay with him always.

Deehan believes that success and recognition can depend as much on those around you as it does on you. He feels he was desperately close to a full international breakthrough . . . then made the wrong transfer move and found his world falling apart.

"I reached my playing peak between 20 and 22 and unfortunately this was the time I was about to leave Aston Villa, my first club, for West Bromwich Albion.

"Both clubs are Birmingham based but for the difference it made to my career I might as well have moved across the world. It was a wrong move.

"I guess the style of play at Albion simply did not suit my game. My standards dropped, my form deteriorated and I felt miserable, for me and the fans who obviously expected a bigger goal-return from me.

"Yet at Villa, playing in the same side as Andy Gray and Brian Little, I found my goal touch quickly and we were a formidable strike-force. In the League alone I hit 42 goals in 110 appearances and that's a goal in every two and a half games! But at Albion I managed only five League goals in just short of 50 full games. Some difference.

"I made no fewer than 11 appearances for the England Under-21s and wanted to go all the way. Lads such as Tony Woodcock and Laurie Cunningham played for the Under-21s at the same time and they progressed.

"I was really grateful when Ken Brown brought me to Carrow Road. I scored on my debut, at home to eventual Division Two Champions Luton, and went on to score 10 League goals and finish second-top scorer as we won promotion.

"I'd knocked in another 10 in the First Division before Christmas and it made me wonder how things would have turned out if I'd made a different move just at that peak time in my career."

RUBBING

Scoring the winning goal in a Cup Final or the one that clinches the Football League Championship is an unforgettable experience, but so can be scoring against former team-mates.

One who has enjoyed that pleasure several times is Aston Villa's powerful striker Peter Withe. He was largely neglected by Southport, Barrow and Wolves before making a name for himself with Birmingham City. Nottingham Forest paid a bargain £42,000 fee for his services in 1976 and he was a star of their Championship-winning side in 1977–78.

His fee shot up to £225,000 when he moved to Newcastle soon after the start of the next season, and Villa paid a club record £½m for his transfer in May 1980. Since then he has led Villa to the League Championship and scored

players who scored memorable goals against their former clubs

the winner in the European Cup Final. Maybe that is Peter's favourite goal, but in the context of this article there are some others which must have given him special pleasure.

How about the winner he scored at Molineux in Villa's League Championship-winning campaign? That reminded Wolves – for whom he played only 17 League games – they should have studied him more closely. Then there was another winning goal for Villa at St. Andrew's the following season, while we shouldn't forget one enjoyable outing last season when he scored two goals in Villa's 4–2 beating of Nottingham Forest. That brought Peter's total of goals against his former clubs in League and Cup to eight.

After only six League games with Villa, young Noel Blake couldn't have been too happy about being transferred to rivals Birmingham City.

So he was extra-pleased to open the scoring against his first club in their 3–0 win last Christmas at St. Andrews.

Bryan Robson scored 39 goals in 197 League appearances for his first club, West Bromwich Albion, and retained his affection for the club following his transfer to Manchester United for a record fee. But that didn't stop him celebrating when he opened the scoring on his old stamping ground of the Hawthorns in September 1982. United led by that goal at half-time, but in the next session Albion struck back with three goals and ruined what could have been a happy memory for Bryan.

How often have Stoke supporters regretted the departure of local discovery Garth Crooks to Spurs? This exciting player failed to score in his first two games against his former club following his £600,000 transfer in 1980, but when Stoke were struggling to

ing for his finest. However, well up in his list of most exciting games was one which gave him immense personal satisfaction. That was the day he scored a hat-trick against the club that first signed him as a professional but let him go without even giving him a chance in the League side. Phil waited a long time to really rub this in but the day came in September 1979 when Southampton beat Derby County 4–0 and Phil got a hat-trick, including one from the penalty spot.

Scoring a hat-trick against one of your old clubs as Phil did is extra-special. But getting one on your former club's own ground is very rare.

In May 1979 when Doncaster Rovers were unsuccessfully struggling to avoid having to apply for re-election, and Grimsby Town were clinching promotion to the Third Division, these two sides met at Blundell Park. The Grimsby supporters were highly delighted that day, not only because their side was about to gain promotion but because the visiting attack was led by an old favourite of theirs, Jack Lewis. In nearly eight seasons with Grimsby Jack had made over 250 League appearances and scored a lot of goals. However, he never played better than in this return to his old stamping ground. No doubt Jack was inspired to be back at Blundell Park for Rovers won a thrilling game 4–3 and Jack Lewis got

Aston Villa's Peter Withe (number nine) scores the winning goal against one of his former clubs, Birmingham City, at St. Andrews in season 1981–82. Bryan Robson (number seven) scores against the club where he began his career. But his joy was short-lived. Manchester United lost 3–1.

avoid relegation in 1982–82 he returned to the Victoria Ground in triumph, scoring both of his side's goals in a 2–0 victory.

Because of local rivalry, games between West Ham and Q.P.R. always have additional interest and in 1979–80 Paul Goddard scored for the Rangers in both games against the Hammers. No wonder then that in the close-season West Ham forked out £800,000 for his transfer. In his first season he repaid that fee by helping the Hammers return to the First Division. He failed to score in his first game against his old club, but in April 1981 Paul more than made up for that by netting a hat-trick for the Hammers in a 3–0 thrashing of Rangers at Upton Park.

Another goalscorer who has moved around is Phil Boyer. He has netted over 150 goals in League games and no doubt would have difficulty in plump-

a hat-trick.

Now that Watford are riding high in the First Division they are not worried about any talent they might have missed along the road, but only last season they were forcefully reminded of one player who spent exactly a year at Vicarage Road but was never given a chance to show his paces in the League side. The player is Gary Donnellan, and you can imagine how overjoyed he was when Reading beat Watford in the Quarter-finals of the League Trophy in December 1982 and Garry scored a hat-trick as well as laying on another goal. Moments like these are cherished long after a player has hung up his boots.

One player with the knack of scoring against his previous club is Mick Robinson of Brighton. The two he got when the seaside club knocked out Manchester City in the Fourth Road of last

Brighton's Mick Robinson has never looked happier than after scoring one of the goals that k.o.'d Manchester City's Cup hopes.

season's F.A. Cup are the ones he'll most treasure.

But Mick is quick to stress that he has no vendetta against the Maine Road club that let him go.

"Outside of Manchester, there's no bigger fan than me," he says. "I was desperately unhappy at leaving Maine Road."

Later, in the Sixth Round, Norwich City's Keith Bertschin scored against one of his previous clubs, Ipswich Town, to end their Wembley dreams. And on the next day, Sunday, Jimmy Case, a one-time Liverpool regular, struck the winning goal to give Brighton their passport to the Sixth Round for the first time ever!

In contrast to the satisfaction and joy most of these players felt scoring against their old club, we have the astonishing story concerning the very last of the 217 League goals scored by Denis Law.

In his scintillating career this lively Scottish international inside-forward scored so many wonderful goals, most of them during eleven glorious years with Manchester United. Then, at the end of 1972–3, he was shocked to be discarded by the club he had helped put at the top of the tree while gaining an F.A. Cup medal and two League Championship medals.

RELUCTANT

Manchester City, with whom he had spent 15 months earlier in his career, immediately invited him back to Maine Road and Denis jumped at the chance, little realising that it was to lead to a most ironical situation.

In the very last game of the season and of his Football League career he lined up against his old mates at Old Trafford.

Denis was reluctant to take part because a victory for City would set the seal on United's first relegation for 37 years. He played because he owed a duty to City, but six minutes from the end it was Denis Law who scored the only goal of the game and one to rank with the finest of his career, back-heeling it into the net!

Instead of feeling overjoyed Denis Law says in his autobiography "I felt sick". Despite his unhappy parting with United he bore his old club no grudge, yet his final goal of his League career not only appeared to send United crashing into the Second Division (as it turned out they would have gone down anyhow with other clubs winning their final games) but also brought disgrace to his old club when the goal brought so many mindless and angry United fans swarming onto the pitch that the referee was forced to abandon the game with five minutes remaining. The League, quite rightly, ordered the result to stand. United had been humiliated – and no one took the tragedy harder than Denis!

OLD **SANTA** CAME TO WATCH US ON SATURDAY

AND WE GAVE HIM SOMETHING TO **THINK** ABOUT

HE THOUGHT HE WAS TOP DOG AT **GIVING THINGS AWAY**

UNTIL HE SAW **OUR DEFENCE**!

My days are numbered! Don't get me wrong, I'm not thinking of quitting just yet. What I mean is the typical centre-half, the dinosaurs of defence, are a dying breed.

They have already become extinct on the Continent. Now the game in Britain has changed and defenders, especially stoppers, have to be more adaptable.

They need 'to be more mobile, quicker off the mark and creative on the ball.

Look at Italy's World Cup winning team in 1982. The two guys at the back, Collovati and Scirea, are destroyers. But they don't just stop opponents. They are play-makers and extremely dangerous on the ball.

Marco Tardelli is one of the toughest defenders in the world, yet he is also a dangerous marksman for Juventus and scored one of Italy's World Cup winning goals against West Germany in the Final.

I bet England manager Bobby Robson would love to call on Arsenal's David O'Leary. I rate the Republic of Ireland number five as the best central defender in Europe.

'Stoppers must be scorers, too!'

—GORDON McQUEEN
MAN. UTD. AND SCOTLAND

Dave's great in the air, his tackles really bite and he's quick and confident.

So is Liverpool's Scottish international Alan Hansen, another of the modern mobile stoppers. Alan is cool, composed and commanding.

For me, though, the outstanding centre-half of all time was Celtic's Billy McNeill, their present manager.

I played against Billy several times when I was with St. Mirren. In those early days I wasn't particularly good at set-pieces. In fact, centre-halves rarely crossed the half-way line.

Billy was one of the first centre-halves to go forward for corner-kicks and dead-ball situations. The tactic was so successful and added so much punch to the team that I resolved to introduce it into my game.

But Billy also could handle tricky Continental centre-forwards as he proved when Celtic beat Inter-Milan to win the European Cup in 1967.

I admire Billy tremendously, but can't say I moulded myself on him or anyone else.

When I was transferred to Leeds United in September 1972, they moulded me into the shape they wanted. I was raw, inexperienced and for the first two years wasn't allowed to run forward.

Don Revie, then manager at Elland Road, ordered me to defend and nothing else until he felt I was confident enough to risk going upfield.

I eventually replaced Jackie Charlton, probably the most outstanding centre-half in English football.

Big Jack was always friendly and particularly helpful when I first arrived at Leeds, but he never actually took me aside and taught me anything. His presence was enough. Like Billy McNeill I learned a great deal just by watching him play.

The finest all-round defender I ever saw was a Leeds team-mate during their successful era during the Seventies . . . Norman Hunter.

If I had a hero then it was Norman, the fiercest competitor I've known in all my years in the game.

But the iron-man of them all was Liverpool's Tommy Smith. Just one look from him was enough to frighten the life out of any player.

Tommy played hard but fair. I never saw him go over the top or set out to deliberately injure an opponent.

Tommy was adaptable and had more football skill than he was often given credit for. Remember his goal for Liverpool in their European Cup Final in 1977 against Borussia Moenchengladbach in Rome? A great header from Steve Heighway's corner was a goal any striker would have been proud to claim.

I've also scored a few goals for Manchester United since signing from Leeds United in February 1978.

In my early days at Old Trafford I was too adventurous. But I still like going forward.

Gordon McQueen — stopper-striker. Perhaps I won't be made redundant after all!

28

'Go out and be special'

That's Malcolm Macdonald's stirring message to all players . . .

The explosive and utterly positive style that made Malcolm Macdonald a centre-forward feared throughout the League has stood him in good stead as a manager, also.

Macdonald blazed a trail of goal-scoring glory at Fulham, Luton, Newcastle and Arsenal, collecting 14 England caps on the way. He was outspoken, critical of those whom he believed were strangling football with negative tactics and always vowed that, should he ever make it as a manager, he would demand a swashbuckling style from his team.

His critics scoffed and said that, once in the dreaded 'hot-seat' Supermac would go the way of the rest and fight to survive.

But he took over from Bobby Campbell at Fulham, having first gone there as commercial manager and rocked the football world by guiding them to promotion from the Third Division in 1982.

And when Fulham were up among the promotion chasers in Division Two the very next season, people began to sit up and take notice . . . because the Londoners, managed by a Fulham-born manager, were attacking their way towards the top.

"Fans want to see goals," said Macdonald: "and we do our best to give them what they want. People love to see shots and headers going in on goal, frantic action in and around the box and their team going flat out for victory. They will forgive you losing if you've given your all. But fans will quickly spot it if you're going through the motions."

And he was full of praise for the youngsters at Craven Cottage who, he believes made his job that much easier.

"When you've got class young players such as Dean Coney and Tony Gale you should not go wrong. I insisted on lighthearted dressing room joking as well as discipline and hard work. The lads responded as I hoped they would. Players are adults and individuals and deserve to be heard when they have something to say. I advocated this, sometimes to my cost, as a player, and I was determined to see this attitude through when I became a manager.

"Give players respect and demand of them that they be professional and you will not be let down. But if you treat your players like schoolboys, you cannot then go wild when they start behaving like schoolboys."

Macdonald's formula is working. He spent his first two years at Fulham building a team without spending money. The fans sensed a change of atmosphere and slowly drifted back. Now it remains to be seen if Macdonald can achieve the very pinnacle with his "Go out and be special" outcry.

Isn't it time we livened up our boring, functional names such as Barnsley, Kilmarnock or Sunderland? The Americans have come up with colourful names Ike Chicago Sting, Tampa Bay Rowdies and Portland Timbers, and they're by no means the only ones. Why can't we have interesting names like Grasshoppers (Switzerland), Hearts of Oak (Ghana), Blackwood Demons (Australia), Racca Rovers (Lesotho), Invincible Eleven (Liberia), Newell's Old Boys (Argentina), Green Buffaloes (Zambia), O'Higgins (Chile), Stationery Stores (Nigeria), Defence Force Eleven (Botswana), St. Joseph's Warriors (Liberia) or Power Dynamos (Zambia)?

C-R-A-Z-Y

Mind you, they sometimes pinch our names – and we could organise a derby between Liverpool (Uruguay) and Everton (Chile) with the winners maybe meeting Arsenal (Egypt) or Mighty Blackpool (Sierra Leone).

And if you fancy Grimsby Grasshoppers, Barnsley Buffaloes or the Roker Rogues, why don't our national teams have nicknames like the Untameable Lions (Cameroon), the Green Eagles (Nigeria) or the Black Stars (Ghana)? How do you fancy the England Elephants, the Scotland Scorpions or the Wales Whales?

Talking about national teams, we could maybe do worse than imitate Somalia, who simply disbanded their side after a grim defeat by Rwanda. Another team to be disbanded was West African champions Police. Everybody got so fed up with them winning the league year after year that the government finally declared them illegal.

Still in Africa, countries like Algeria, Morocco and Tunisia were years ahead of England in giving three points for a win. Unfortunatley they also give two for a draw and one for a defeat, so what's the . . . er . . . point?

By the way, Algeria is one of the countries where football is amateur and transfers are illegal. In Senegal they sometimes don't go down too well either. When international goalkeeper Mansour Wade decided to leave Associated Police Force F.C. to join rivals Jeanne d'Arc, his former team-mates decided to chuck him in jail.

Let's face it, world jails will soon be full of football personnel unless someone puts a stop to all the jiggery-pokery. We've had slush-money scandals in France and Yugoslavia, where someone creams off a percentage of the gate money and stuffs it under a mattress. We've had illegal pools scandals in Italy and Brazil. And there've been bribery scandals at most points between Turkey and Argentina.

In South America three clubs admitted in public that they'd paid 60,000 dollars to rig the Semi-Final draw of the Copa Libertadores – a competition where no holds are barred, and home teams are not beyond doctoring the visitors' food or spiking their drinks with laxatives so that they'll run for the full 90 minutes.

Transfer-seeking 'keeper stuck in jail by team-mates!

Bribery is such a way of life that *three* referees are nominated for big games – on the grounds that it's more difficult and more expensive to bribe three men than one. Shortly before the kick-off, the Three Just Men draw lots and the winner referees the match while the other two run the lines.

In Colombia the bribery situation reached such proportions that they started importing foreign referees – and 24 hours before big games, all the weekend's referees are whisked off to a mountain hideaway where there isn't even a phone. That way, no one knows who's going to handle each match until the man in black turns up at the ground.

Mind you, referees are given a rough time in Spain as well. All match reports include a section where the ref's performance is analysed with a massive magnifying-glass. What's more, if he doesn't take the fancy of club directors, they can have him banned from refereeing their team. Some refs are banned by so many clubs that they have trouble getting a game, and the average Spanish referee handles no more than 14 games a season. Then they're slated for being unfit and out of practice . . .

The only people who can't criticise refs are players and managers – unless they fancy a charge of bringing the game into disrepute. In Greece, British coach Les Shannon was hauled across the coals for calling an official a "drag artist". Rumour has it that the referee then hit him with his handbag in the dressing-room!

Talking about dressing-rooms, they don't get a great deal of use in some Africa countries. Visiting players often prefer to remain on the pitch at half-time, as it has been known for the odd witch-doctor to slip into the dressing-room and deposit a few "gri-gris" aimed at putting the kybosh on the visitors' key players.

Even that didn't work during a

WORLD

In Colombia, no one knows who'll referee a game until he turns up!

SAPORITO

continental clash at Bamako, and a win for the visitors provoked a Cabinet Minister and his entourage to burst into the dressing-rooms and give the referee a right royal sorting-out – which later earned him a life ban.

Talking about life bans, Australian players still hold the whip-hand, with assaults on referees top of the list of heinous crimes.

When they staged the World Youth Tournament out there, Cameroon played well, and three players decided to cash-in on their success in a big way. Each went home and signed for three different clubs at the same time, pocketing a nice signing-on fee from all three.

Doubling and trebling-up is a way of life in Chilean football, where attendances dropped so far that they play two or three league games one after the other in the same stadium, to minimise organisation costs. Fans enter the ground for a 3 o'clock kick-off and come out at a quarter to nine.

Down in Argentina, Racing Club haven't played a home game for years, as their stadium at Avellaneda is falling to bits. They use the Boca Juniors ground instead.

It's amazing that some footballers find time to play football. Soccer-mad Brazil is famous for its hordes of press, radio and TV reporters, and mega-star Zico reckons he gives 3,000 interviews

a year. Couldn't he hire a double?

With regard to commentaries, the South Americans take the biscuit when it comes to shouting "GOOOOOOOOOOOOOOOL!!!".

In fact, if goals are the life and soul of football, David Coleman's nonchalant 'One-nil" must have been inspired by an undertaker.

He could take lessons from the Colombian radio commentator at the

Atletico Junior – Nacional game. When Junior scored, he threw back his head, shut his eyes and launched himself into a shout that lasted 36 seconds. When he opened his eyes, he was aghast to find that the goal had been disallowed, and listeners then heard sounds of the microphone being hurled to the floor and heavy footsteps storming out of the cabin, never to return.

A little further north, Honduras may have fogotten their soccer war with El Salvador in 1969, but they've more recently got themselves thrown out of the World Youth Tournament for fielding over-age players. They've been doing it since 1977, when half the side was anything up to five years over the limit – with the result that many Honduran internationals turn up from time to time with different birth dates. 1982 World Cup star Anthony Costly, for example, is registered with FIFA as having been born on December 13th, 1954, November 13th, 1957 and November 12th, 1959, which means he annually breaks the world record for birthday presents.

And who would have thought that the Honduras team would include a black, cricket-loving striker called Jimmy Bailey who dreams of playing at Lords?

Mind you, even the USA mysteriously managed to nationalise a Uruguayan striker, Tabare Ramos, just 24 hours before the World Youth eliminators – and he responded with vital goals against Puerto Rico and Guatemala.

At least the Americans are the journalist's dream, with their huge bundles of helpful Public Relations hand-outs. What's more, they're in English – or something like it. Did you realise, for example, that "the Semi-Final round will pair the highest-ranked Quarter-Final winner against the lowest-ranked survivor in one series and the remaining two winners in the other. Again it will be two-out-of-three with the higher-ranked team holding the home field edge."

Ah . . . at the present moment in time and slanted in the long-term projection mode, soccer shows an on-going zany situation . . .

Brazilian star Zico gives 3,000 interviews a year!

SAPORITO

31

DAZZLER DANNY

One clear sign of a good player is the buzz of excitement that goes up from the crowd whenever he receives the ball.

Such excitement is usually generated by midfield players or strikers. But in the case of Coventry right-back Danny Thomas you must make an exception.

The Worksop-born defender really blossomed when Dave Sexton succeeded Gordon Milne at Highfield Road in May, 1981. Sexton, who was also manager of the England Under 21-team at the time, quickly included the 5′ 7″ Thomas in his European Under-21 Championship squad, and reaped instant dividends.

Thomas was an integral part of the England side that beat West Germany in a memorable two-legged final and signalled to the rest of Europe that he is one of the most skilful and exciting of the new breed of full-backs emerging from England.

"That seems an age ago now," recalled Thomas: "but it gave me a taste for international football that has grown virtually every month.

POWERFUL SHOT

"Working for Dave Sexton is a gret help because he demands hard work and discipline from his players without ever detracting from their skills. He wants the game to be a spectacle and encourages individual skills.

"That is why I am encouraged to get forward, take up attacking positions and supporting positions on the right and expected to supply a percentage of good and accurate crosses."

Thomas has a powerful shot in that right foot, as a few goalkeepers will testify and has already made his mark with some excellent goals.

"But first and foremost I am a defender whose job it is to shut out any dangerous opponent down my wing. I appreciate the importance of priorities and my first priority is to be an effective defender."

But it's those surging runs up the line that get the fans on their feet as Thomas exhibits confidence and skill on the ball. He can take on an opponent like a true winger or whip in a deep angled cross to catch a defence back-tracking . . . and still recover in time to shut out danger on the break.

Small wonder that Sexton considers him priceless . . . and many in the game predict that Danny Thomas may one day achieve for the senior England side what his skill and pace have done for the Under-21's.

Kenny and his team-mates celebrate at the end of the 1981-82 season. Liverpool had won the championship for a record 13th time.

"I've been very lucky in my career. Few injuries and always playing in good sides. Few lads are that fortunate, especially over a long career.

"The occasional setback makes you all the more appreciative of success and providing that hunger is sustained then opponents eventually have to retreat. But that is no secret. We are on television as often, if not more often, than most sides. So how can we have any secrets? No, it's all about dedication, hard work and the will to succeed.

"And if you ask any Liverpool player you will find that his will to succeed comes across immediately."

'NO SECRET BEHIND LIVERPOOL'S SUCCESS'

says Kenny Dalglish

Kenny Dalglish is probably the only player in Britain who could match his own weight in medals and awards.

Liverpool's prolific goalscoring Scot has already swept the board more than once while playing for Celtic and now stands shin-pads deep in silverware after six and a half years of incredible Anfield glory.

But while most people with such an astonishing success record would take every available opportunity to boast about their achievements, the quietly-spoken Dalglish chooses to remind you that no one player can win anything without the help of ten others.

"People ask me what is the secret of Liverpool's success," said Dalglish. "But in all honesty there is no secret.

"The work behind the scenes never stops. We operate on a squad system and every player knows that if he does not reach and maintain the high standards of fitness and discipline demanded by the management then there is someone waiting in the wings to take his place.

"Teams have come and gone at Anfield. Many players have played in more than one particular era. But always there is the knowledge that someone is pushing you for a place in the line-up, no matter who you are.

"It's a collective hunger for success that drives us on. No matter how many medals I win, no one medal is quite as good as the very next one! The only thing that can put a smile on my face is ending a hard, demanding season with something to show for it.

'MILLION POUND' SUB.

Labelled a flop by Newcastle, Mark McGhee had everything to prove when he joined Aberdeen for a cut-price £60,000 several seasons ago.

And, just to make things even tougher, a season later he was told he was going to fill the boots of Steve Archibald after the Pittodrie prince of the penalty-area took his flashing talents to Spurs in exchange for a near-£1 million cheque.

But mighty McGhee accepted the challenge and he won the Players' Player of the Year award that season.

"It meant I was doing my job properly," says McGhee. "After all, these were the players I was facing week in, week out."

McGhee proved more than capable of taking over the main striking role vacated by Archibald and, in true storybook fashion, he ended the season as Aberdeen's top goal-scorer and one of the most consistent marksmen in Scotland.

SCOTLAND CALL-UP

There was even talk of a possible international call-up by Jock Stein, but that didn't materialise. McGhee realises only too well soccer is a strange game. He kicked off his career with Bristol City, but left Ashton Gate as a teenager because he was homesick.

He returned to Scotland and Celtic's former boss Jock Stein offered him trials at Parkhead. Stein was certainly impressed, but fate stepped in and robbed McGhee of his opportunity of playing in the famed green-and-white.

Stein was involved in a car crash and while he spent a season recuperating, McGhee drifted out of the Parkhead picture and was eventually signed by Morton.

His career really took off at Cappielow and after a storm of goals he went to Newcastle in a £150,000 deal. Sadly, the St. James's Park club were in dire trouble when McGhee arrived and he never claimed a permanent first team place.

Another twist arrived when Aberdeen manager Alex Ferguson came on the scene.

"Life has been good since then." says McGhee. "Aberdeen are a fabulous club. I wish I had joined them years before I did. I really enjoy my football at Pittodrie."

Watford's Ross Jenkins shadowed by Sunderland's Rob Hindmarch.

35

Anyone who doesn't believe that the crowd can have an effect on how the game is played has never been to a local derby. Obviously there is the burning ambition among the players to do well against their neighbours from down the road, but the fact that these games attract bigger than average attendances adds so much to the atmosphere.

Take the special brand of rivalry that exists between Arsenal and Spurs, a rivalry which stretches back over more than 90 League games, never mind their clashes in other competitions.

For sheer nail-biting tension there has been nothing to excel that Monday evening game at White Hart Lane in May 1971. It was the last game of the season, and Leeds United at the top of the table had completed their programme and were one point above Arsenal. The Gunners knew that to win the League Championship they had to either beat Spurs or force a goalless draw. The position was so tight that a 1-1 draw would have meant Arsenal missing the trophy on goal average.

There were just under 52,000 inside White Hart Lane and, with the gates closed half an hour before kick-off, nearly as many locked out.

They're fan-tastic
DERBY DAYS

With two minutes to go there was still no score, but in one of the most thrilling climaxes ever seen for the League Championship, never mind a local derby game, up popped Ray Kennedy to head the winner off the bar after Pat Jennings had pushed out a header from John Radford. Arsenal survived last ditch efforts by Spurs to equalise, and only five days later Arsenal completed the "double" by

coming from behind to beat Liverpool in extra-time in the F.A. Cup Final.

That's just one of the series of North London derbies. For more thrills we could recall any of the three games between these two clubs which have resulted in 4-4 draws – February 1958, October 1962, and October 1963. In the first at Highbury, Arsenal held the lead until two goals in a minute by Tommy Harmer (pen.) and Bobby Smith made it a draw. Spurs led 4-2 in the 1962 game at White Hart Lane which was a personal triumph for George Eastham and also an unknown 18-year-old, David Court, brought into the Arsenal side in place of their injured £70,000 centre-forward, Joe Baker. David scored twice. 12 months later at Highbury Spurs were again leading 4-2 but Arsenal levelled the score after the interval. On this occasion George Eastham got a couple while the burly Bobby Smith also scored two for the Spurs.

While Arsenal and Spurs have had some really vicious clashes Liverpool and Everton have, with few exceptions, developed a tradition of sportsmanlike encounters, a comment which surprises a lot of fans who have not

had the pleasure of watching any of these games. Few readers will recall Liverpool's 7-4 win over Everton at Anfield back in 1933 when The Reds were leading 3-2 at the interval but piled it on in the second half with Harold Barton completing a hat-trick. The inimitable Dixie Dean also got his usual couple for Everton that day.

ONLY DEFEAT

More will recall the shock result in December 1969 when The Reds gained their first victory at Goodison in eight League visits, scoring three without reply through Emlyn Hughes, Sandy Brown (o.g.), and Bobby Graham, all of them in the second-half. Everton were already at the top of the table at that time and went on to win the Championship. This was their only home defeat that season, indeed, it was to be their only defeat in a run of 39 home League games.

We don't even need to go back that far to recall another thriller in this particular series. In October, 1980, when Liverpool visited Everton The Blues went into a 2-goal lead through Asa Hartford and Joe McBride, but Liverpool fought back in breathtaking fashion to draw with Sammy Lee and Kenny Dalglish doing the honours.

Even though the Sheffield clubs have rather slipped from the limelight

Ray Kennedy scores the goal that set Arsenal on the road to the "double" in 1971.

Everton's Joe McBride gets the goal that put his club 2-0 up against Liverpool.

Wilkinson. Things got so hot that the referee had to call a halt and have a word with both captains, but although outplayed Wednesday proved in this game that it is goals that count. Despite playing the classier football United could not find the net, although they didn't allow Wednesday to improve on their two goals.

Moving over to Manchester we have an impossible choice from well over 100 League and Cup derbies. However, we don't have to go back very far for one of the biggest shocks. That was early in 1980-81 when City made such a disastrous start and were without a win after seven games. Their eighth was a visit to Old Trafford. Twice that afternoon the 56,000 crowd saw United go ahead, but each time City levelled the score and it ended all square at 2-2. Steve Coppell and Arthur Albiston scored for United while Kevin Reeves and Roger Palmer got the equalisers.

LEVEL PEGGING

Remember the season when Manchester City first won the League Cup – 1969-70. They met United in the two-leg Semi-Finals before beating W.B.A. at Wembley after extra-time. In the first-leg at Maine Road City won by the odd goal in three, a Francis Lee penalty. In the second-leg at Old Trafford City again surprised United by holding them to a 2-2 draw. There was

December 1908 must be included in any story of local derbies. Such a score would be a shock at any time, but this was at St. James' Park, and as an away win it has been equalled but never been excelled in the First Division.

Over at Nottingham the two local first-class clubs have been battling away in various competitions for over a century and County supporters must have been really excited when their favourites played their first Division One game against the Forest for 57 years and won 2-0. That was in January 1982 and it was at the City Ground too. Paul Hooks and Trevor Christie got the goals in this historic game, both of them in the second-half.

With Forest taking most of the limelight in recent years the result may seem surprising, but actually it was County's seventh win in eight League visits to the City Ground.

All the local derbies we have mentioned have been something special because of that extra bit of needle, but nowhere is the brand of competition so keen than it is between the Old Firm of Celtic and Rangers up in Glasgow. They have met in over 180 League games. To these we must add all of their clashes in the Scottish Cup, League Cup, Glasgow Cup and Glasgow Charity Cup, making a total of well over 300 games. Take your choice from that! One thing you can be sure of is that everyone of those games was played in a unique atmosphere, for no matter what the standard of play the mere fact that these two clubs are meeting each other is enough to excite their spectators.

Ignoring the dim, distant past when Celtic beat Rangers 5-3 at Parkhead in 1894-95, or Rangers' 4-3 victory on the same ground in 1935-36, and determined to remain neutral, we must recall one victory for either side.

In September 1971 Celtic were 2-1 down in the interval at Ibrox, but fought back so well that they ran out 3-2 winners with Jimmy Johnstone heading the winner in the last minute.

The Rangers victory we want to recall was the one that brought them the Scottish Cup for the 19th time in 1965-66. Celtic were clear favourites to win and the tension and excitement was drawn out over two games. The first resulted in a goalless draw, and the replay, four days later, looked like ending the same way. Then, however, came the reason for mentioning this particular encounter – one of the greatest goals ever scored by a Ranger and the first Scandinavian to capture a Scottish Cup medal – Kai Johansen.

There were only 10 minutes remaining and the ball was being cleared from the Celtic goalmouth when up charged this Rangers full-back. Without hesitation he took it in his stride and his crashing first-time shot from 20 yards out left Ronnie Simpson in the Celtic goal diving hopelessly as the ball nearly took the back out of the net. How valiantly Celtic battled for an equaliser in the closing minutes when the excitement reached fever pitch, but Rangers held them at bay. The Hampden Roar that evening matched anything heard before or since, and local derbies everywhere are known for straining the vocal chords.

for a spell in recent years we could not ignore this cradle of our national game when discussing local derbies. Don't forget that when Wednesday and United met at Hillsborough on Boxing Day 1979 they attracted a record Third Division crowd of 49,309. Some indication of the special attraction of a local derby. However, Wednesday won 4-0 that day when it was too much one way traffic to make it really interesting for both sets of supporters.

Back in March, 1960, however, when Wednesday visited Bramall Lane in a sixth Round F.A. Cup-tie, United outclassed Wednesday, especially in the first-half, yet the visitors led 2-0 at the interval, both goals being scored with cracking shots from Derek

Man. City's Roger Palmer levels in a Manchester derby game.

a crowd of 63,000 at this game and it was level pegging all the way, Paul Edwards putting United ahead but Ian Bowyer equalising before the interval. In the second-half fortunes again ran from end to end with Denis Law getting one for United and Mike Summerbee scoring City's second goal.

Breaking away to the North-East for a moment there is little doubt about the most memorable game between Newcastle United and Sunderland. Although it was so one-sided with Sunderland winning 9-1, this game, in

TOP MARK

Young Mark Chamberlain of Stoke has the same ability as his famous predecessor – Sir Stanley Matthews – to mesmerise defenders with his magical ball skills.

In fact, he has been hailed as the black version of the former Stoke and England winger of the Fifties who was acknowledged as a great match-winner and crowd-puller. Mark, born in the Potteries of Jamaican parents, could also become a soccer legend.

Not for him the luxury of graduating from the apprentices at a First Division club. Mark started the hard way, with Fourth Division Port Vale. Stoke's manager, Richie Barker, brought him to the Victoria Ground for a bargain £120,000. Since then, Mark has become an established First Division player and played at full level for England. He had a dream debut, coming on as substitute against Luxembourg at Wembley and scoring a fine goal in his country's record 9–0 win.

Luton Town's Paul Walsh about to be tackled by Spurs' Glenn Hoddle.

HOW ABOUT

In full internationals England's longest run without defeat was one of 20 games (won 16, drawn 4) between April 1889 and April 1896. In games played since World War Two the longest run is 19 games (won 16, drawn 3) between losing 3-2 to Austria at Wembley in October, 1965, and losing by the same score, and on the same ground, to Scotland in April, 1967. This, of course, was England's World Cup-winning team.

The only goalkeeper ever to score on his debut in British first-class football was Belgian-born Mark De Clerek. He scored for Aberdeen with a long clearance against Berwick Rangers in the Scottish League Cup on August 31st, 1980.

In the F.A. Cup Semi-Finals of 1961 Leicester City and Sheffield United played for 4 hours 17 minutes before Jimmy Walsh (Leicester) broke the stalemate with the first goal. That is the longest time in an F.A. Cup Semi-Final without a goal being scored. Leicester went on to win this second replay 2-0.

Huddersfield Town once enjoyed a run of 19 years without losing an F.A. Cup tie on their own ground. It was ironic that this remarkable run should be brought to an end in February, 1932, by a player who seldom scored goals – Herbie Roberts, the famous "stopper" centre-half. He headed the only goal in an Arsenal victory at Leeds Road.

One of the finest feats of goalscoring in Scottish post-war League football was that by Henry Morris in 1947-48 when he netted 41 goals in only 29 appearances for East Fife in the Second Division. That season East Fife finished 11 points ahead of their nearest rivals with a bag of 103 goals, losing only two of their 30 games.

Lawrie McMenemy was the first manager to steer two different clubs to the Championship of the Fourth Division – Doncaster Rovers in 1968-69 and Grimsby Town in 1971-72. This feat has since been performed by Dave Smith – Mansfield Town 1974-75, Southend United 1980-81, and Graham Taylor – Lincoln City 1975-76 and Watford 1977-78. In view of this it is remarkable that no manager has ever achieved a similar distinction in the present Third Division.

Leicester City is the only club to have suffered relegation just one season after promotion to the First Division on as many as three occasions. The three seasons in which they won promotion to be relegated 12 months later were 1907-08, 1953-54, and 1979-80.

In 1891 an England v Scotland international at Blackburn was boycotted by thousands of local fans because no Blackburn Rovers player had been selected. It was more than

Arsenal's Herbie Roberts' goal ended Huddersfield's series of Cup-tie wins.

local prejudice for the "Athletic News" commented that the exclusion of Rovers stars, Southworth and Barton, was an injustice both to the players and to England. England won 2-1 and strangely enough the winner was scored by a native of Blackburn, Edgar Chadwick, who was then with Everton.

In season 1912-13 when Woolwich Arsenal created a First Division record low by scoring a mere 26 goals, their top scorer, C. E. Randall, scored only four goals. Leicester City equalled this dismal record as recently as 1977-78 when they totalled 26 goals while playing four more First Division games than Woolwich Arsenal had done. Their top scorer, Geoff Salmons, also got four goals. Naturally both these sides suffered relegation.

Action from a goalless First Division game in Season 1977-78 between Leicester and Leeds. Leicester were relegated after equalling a low-scoring record.

Among club goalscoring records for an individual in a single season in either the Premier or First Divisions of the Scottish League the most recent was created by Blair Miller when he scored 28 First Division goals for Clydebank in 1978-79. That season Miller got off to a great start by scoring in each of his side's first seven games.

Celtic were caught up in a rush of fixtures at the end of season 1915-16 and had to play two Scottish League games on the same day. They beat Raith Rovers 6-0 before travelling to Fir Park where they defeated Motherwell 3-1. Celtic easily won the Championship that season.

When West Bromwich Albion were due to play at Walsall in the F.A. Cup First Round in 1899-1900 they sent their office boy to measure the Fellows Park pitch believing it to be shorter than regulations permitted. Their suspicions were confirmed, but the Albion decided to reserve any protest they might make in case they lost the tie. Walsall, however, got wind of the situation and had their pitch lengthened in time for the kick-off. The result was a draw 1-1, but Albion easily won the replay 6-1.

Benfica 0, Ealing Association 3. No, not really such a shock result for it happened in April 1914 when the London club was among soccer pioneers who toured Portugal.

When Oldham Athletic's left-back, Billy Cook, refused to leave the field after being ordered off in a First Division game at Middlesbrough the referee abandoned the proceedings. Middlesbrough were leading 4-1 at the time and the Football League ruled that the result should stand. Cook received 12 months suspension. The date of this debacle was April 3rd 1915.

The famous Irish international George Best once appeared in all four home countries in a period of 10

THAT? Fantastic Facts to make your eyes pop...

days – Northern Ireland v. Iceland, Belfast, September 21st 1977; Fulham at Cardiff in Football League, September 24th; Fulham at St. Mirren, Anglo Scottish Cup, September 26th, and Fulham at Crystal Palace, Football League, October 1st. Ironically, the great man never represented his country in the World Cup Finals.

After making four League appearances for Notts County there was a gap of nearly 10 years before forward John L. Froggatt next appeared in the League with Colchester United. Froggatt then went on to play in over

200 Football League games with Colchester United, Port Vale and Northampton Town. John's last appearance for Notts County was in October 1964 and his first for Colchester was not until August 1974.

In the Scottish League Airdrieonians were undefeated at home in a run of 61 games between September 23rd, 1922, and December 5th, 1925, when they lost 2-1 to Morton.

The only newcomer to Division One to win the League Championship in their very first season after promotion was Ipswich Town in 1961-62. The next best position for a newcomer to the First Division was achieved by Bristol City when they were runners-up in 1906-07.

When playing for Celtic v Aberdeen in a Scottish League game, September 26th, 1953, Bobby Collins scored all of Celtic's goals in a 3-0 victory from the penalty-spot. Bobby subsequently became well-known in the Football League where he appeared for Everton, Leeds United, Bury and Oldham Athletic.

Five teams have gone through a season of Football League matches without collecting a single point away from home – Northwich Victoria in 1893-94, Crewe Alexandra in 1894-95, Loughborough Town in 1899-1900, Doncaster Rovers in 1904-05, and

Nelson in 1930-31. The last named did so in Division Three (N) while the others were all in Division Two.

The first F.A. Cup Final at which any part of the game was televised was Sunderland v Preston North End in 1937.

Alfie Conn has the unique distinction of collecting a Scottish Cup winner's medal with Rangers when they beat Celtic in 1973, and also with Celtic when they defeated Rangers in 1977. Conn also won caps for Scotland between these periods at Spurs.

(Above) The first F.A. Cup Final to be partly televised – Sunderland v Preston in 1937. Sunderland won 3-1. (Right) Jimmy Greaves was top scorer in the First Division for three successive seasons.

There has only been one Football League game in which a side has scored as many as six goals and still lost. This was in the Second Division December 21st, 1957, when Charlton Athletic met Huddersfield Town at The Valley. With half an hour to go Huddersfield were leading 5-1 but the final result was a 7-6 victory for Charlton. This was the game in which Johnny Summers scored five for Charlton.

Although Middlesbrough scored more goals than any other side in the First Division in 1937-38 (80) they were relegated. Their wins that season included 6-1(h) and 7-1(a) v. Derby County, 7-1(h) v. W.B.A., and 7-2(h) v. Leeds United. 80 is still the highest number of goals scored by a side relegated from the First Division.

Jimmy Greaves is the only player ever to have topped the First Division goalscoring list in three successive seasons. While he was with Spurs he headed the list in 1962-63 (37 goals), 1963-64 (35 goals), and 1964-65 (29 goals). In that last season he actually shared top place with Andy McEvoy of Blackburn Rovers. Jimmy

Greaves also created the post-war First Division record with 41 goals for Chelsea in 1960-61.

Alex Elder won a League Championship medal and gained his first full international cap for N. Ireland in his initial Football League season. This was with Burnely in 1959-60. He later played for Stoke.

Billy Horton of Aldershot had played in both the F.A. Cup and the Football League Cup before he made his Football League debut in 1962-63.

Because of the bad weather during the winter of season 1978-79 the Scottish Cup Second Round tie between Inverness Thistle and Falkirk, due to be played on January 6th, was completed at the 30th attempt on February 22nd when Falkirk won 4-0.

Goalkeeper Jim Barron (Oxford United) was booked by referee David Wallace **before** the Second Division game with Blackpool began, August 21st 1968, for making a mark on the 6-yard line.

Referee M. A. Fussey had to recall the teams after discovering he had ended the Bolton Wanderers v. Blackburn Rovers Second Division game six minutes too early – February 3rd, 1968. This is not the only instance of its kind.

In a First Division game, September 18th, 1957, Aston Villa beat Leicester City 5-1 at Villa Park. In the return game that season Leicester won 6-1. Oddly enough there was a similar turnabout between the same two clubs back in 1934-35. Then Leicester's 5-0 victory against Villa at Filbert Street was followed by a 5-0 defeat at Villa Park.

Being England's undisputed first-choice 'keeper has not added to the pressures of superstar goalkeeper Peter Shilton . . . in fact the opposite applies.

It took Shilton a long time to get into that position after years of intense – but never bitter – rivalry with Ray Clemence.

And having achieved that status, Shilton is determined to enjoy it.

He reveals: "It's a great feeling to know that you are recognised as number one and it gives you the right kind of enthusiasm and confidence for going about your job.

"When people are saying nice things about you – as Bobby Robson has about me since he took over the England management – it is bound to give you a lift.

"I've waited a long time to get into the position and obviously I want it to stay that way. Any professional foot-

playing First Division football until I'm 40. If I'm playing for England then, so much the better.

"To be honest, it's a target that I can see me reaching. I'm as fit as I have ever been; I look after myself, train hard and see no problems ahead.

"I've got a contract with Southampton until the end of the next World Cup in 1986. That's far enough into the future to be thinking about but I've always been ambitious and I don't see any harm in wanting to be around the First Division on my 40th birthday.

orities are not careful they will take away too many dimensions from our work.

"When I kept goal for England in Denmark last year, the referee insisted that I got rid of the ball not just in four steps but within four seconds. Things like that need to be sorted out otherwise goalkeepers won't know which way they are going."

But even in the most complicated set of circumstances, it's difficult to imagine Peter Shilton going any way but the right one.

PETER SHILTON

baller should want to be the best at his job . . . and I'm no different.

"There's enormous satisfaction to be had from being first choice at anything and I'm sure it hasn't affected me one bit since I got the job on the eve of the World Cup."

Shilton's claim is substantiated not only in the superlatives that Ron Greenwood and Bobby Robson have heaped on him but in the cold statistics that go hand in hand with goalkeeping.

And there can be no better yardstick of Shilton's ability than in the record he brought back with him from Spain. Just one goal conceded in five games against France, Czechoslovakia, Kuwait, West Germany and Spain speaks for itself.

Those kind of individual displays left Clemence in the background but despite the shift in status for the two goalkeepers, their relationship stays the same.

Adds Shilton: "When Ray and I were having alternate games, I don't think either of us was totally pleased about the situation but realised that it was better to get one game in two than none at all.

"And although I got the shirt on a regular basis last year nothing changed between us. We are both professionals and accept the situation as it applies at any time.

"I can perhaps understand his position better than he could mine a few years earlier when he was preferred in Don Revie's reign as England manager.

"I knew how I felt at that time so I've got the fullest understanding about the way Ray felt when our roles were reversed. The only hope is that we are still around contesting the England jersey for many more years to come."

He argues: "I'm 33 now and I don't see any reason why I should not be

"It's important to have fresh challenges, however, and that's why I made the move from Nottingham Forest to Southampton last year.

"I had a marvellous time with Brian Clough and Peter Taylor in Nottingham. They were good for me and I think I was good for them . . . and I've got a lot of trophies at home to prove it.

"But I think the time had come for me to move on from Forest and take on something new. And although things didn't go too well at the start at Southampton, there's a new, young team taking shape there as well as there is at Forest.

CONFIDENT

"When I went to Southampton, it was as if I was the last part of the jigsaw. They had Kevin Keegan and a team that didn't seem to be far away from winning something . . . but Kevin left and it took time for a new team to take shape.

"There are a lot of good young players at Southampton, the management is right and I'm confident about the future at The Dell. It's certainly a nice place to be.

"I know I had my work cut out when I first went there and for several games I had probably more work to do than I have ever had in my career.

"But that was an indication of the way the game has become more entertaining in recent years.

"Players are being encouraged to get forward more, more chances are being created and as a consequence goalkeepers are having their work cut out. I'm not complaining about that because goalkeepers generally like to be involved.

"A few things have gone against goalkeepers in recent years like the severe punishment for handling outside the area and if the soccer auth-

Peter's safe hands foil a Spanish attack in the goalless draw against the host nation in the 1982 World Cup Finals.

'I can play First Division football until I'm 40 — and also be in goal for England in the next World Cup . . .'

England's Number One

Gordon in full flight is confronted by Southampton's David Armstrong.

HIS OWN BIGGEST CRITIC

thats Villa's Gordon Cowans

Self criticism is the key to the character of Gordon Cowans. Aston Villa's former England Under 21 midfield skipper sets himself very high standards, and when he fails to meet them, hammers himself harder than anyone else ever has.

Team-mates and opponents alike share a respect and admiration for Villa's wiry, skilful play-maker. They talk of his courage, his energy, vision and hatred of losing.

At 25, Cowans can boast a League Championship medal and a European Cup winner's medal as well as his honours at various levels for England.

But he is still a modest young man who insists that without the right men around it is impossible to shine.

"I have enjoyed some great seasons for Villa," he said: "the European Cup year, for example. I played in all 42 League games and emerged with 11 League and Cup goals. I know I did a good job overall . . . yet we finished 11th in the table.

"I played my part in our march to beating Bayern Munich in that memorable European Cup Final in Rotterdam in 1982, a real night to remember.

"Bayern began as favourites and they did boast a powerful side. But despite losing Jimmy Rimmer after only nine minutes young Nigel Spink played out of his skin as substitute 'keeper and Peter Withe's close-range shot flew in off the left hand post to give us a memorable 1–0 victory, against all odds.

"Yet the year we really put Villa back on the map by winning the League title – the first time it had come to Villa Park since 1910 – I also played in all 42 games, but for me it was a bitterly disappointing season.

"I scored only five goals and I was not happy with my passing. I worked very hard to make up for this and did my fair share of grafting. But the game is about much more than that to me, and I understood perfectly why my then international chances blew out the window only a few months after being Under-21 skipper and playing for the England B side.

"I was giving the ball away and yet I consider passing my greatest strength! Now I can appreciate the importance of personal satisfaction. I was very happy for the lads and for our great supporters. But I could not kid myself into believing that I'd had a great season just because of that medal."

Such biting self-analysis is the reason behind Cowans' abiity to sustain such a high standard of consistency, even when things are not going right on the pitch.

"We blew out of the title hunt again in 1982-83, failed to capture that elusive World Club Championship title when Penerol of Uruguay beat us 2-0 and ended up caught between too many trophies because we were still defending our European title.

"But whether I have a medal at the end of a season or not I do not use it as my yardstick. I look in the mirror and admit to what I know deep down. That way I can look everyone in the eye on good days and say I'm doing well."

TONY WOODCOCK ENGLAND STRIKER
MADE IN WEST GERMANY!

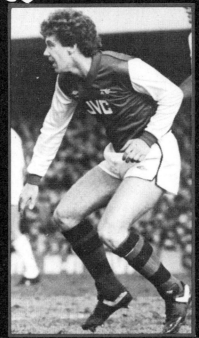

Arsenal and England striker Tony Woodcock is very proud of the reputation he has earned in the First Division as the most dangerous "foreign" player at Highbury.

The arrival of Yugoslavian international Vladimir Petrovic gave Arsenal a whole new dimension and went a long way towards appeasing those fans who still have not forgiven Arsenal for allowing Liam Brady to leave.

But it's been the sharpness and instinctive positional play of Woodcock that has made him a hero in North London, initially at a time when Arsenal's fortunes were decidedly average.

And even Woodcock himself admits that he had to leave England and the glory days of Brian Clough's Nottingham Forest to improve as a player.

"At Forest I enjoyed a tremendous partnership with Garry Birtles and we won memorable honours. But when I joined Cologne in the Bundesliga I discovered what playing with your back to goal is all about," he said.

"Football League defenders mark you when you enter their area or zone of the pitch, they pick you up as you approach their goal. But you have a certain amount of room to work, even then.

"But the German League is so tight that you have to sharpen up all your reflexes or fail. I worked hard during my two and a half years out there and believe it made me a better player."

Hence the "foreign" tag. Because without the strictures of man-to-man marking Woodcock is now a very dangerous handful for any British defence. Just like Kevin Keegan, who returned from Hamburg to a certain amount of scepticism . . . and scored 30 goals for Southampton, Woodcock has benefitted from his stay on the Continent.

"Some of the top West German defenders are really the best in the world. I remember seeing Bertie Vogts in action and my own most vivid memory is of Borussia Moenchengladbach's Lothar Matthaus.

"He always became my personal shadow when Cologne played his side. Lothar is a fine player on the ball and uses it well. But his real talent was disciplined man to man marking. And he could drive you up the wall.

"He would snap around my heels for the full 90 minutes and it was virtually impossible to catch him dozing or lose him. When you learn to cope with that type of strong, tight defensive play and still find the net, playing back in England is all the more enjoyable."

Arsenal and England have certainly reaped the benefit of their prolific and gifted "foreign" import.

Playing for Cologne, Tony learnt how to cope with man-to-man marking.

PLAY ANYWHERE CAPTAIN

When it comes to versatility in soccer Glasgow Rangers' Northern Ireland international star John McClelland surely has everyone licked.

"I've played senior football in my home country, Wales, England and now Scotland," says the likeable McClelland, appointed skipper of the world-famous Ibrox side last season.

"That was a real honour," he says. "I was surprised when John Greig offered me the job, but I accepted right away. It meant so much to me."

McClelland's versatility isn't just confined to playing soccer in all four home countries . . . he's also moved around the team to fill a few departments in his time.

"I've played in defence and midfield for Northern Ireland," says McClelland, who was a giant in Billy Bingham's rearguard during their mesmerising World Cup Finals in Spain in '82.

"It's the same with Rangers — I've played in a few positions for them, too. I've had roles in central defence as well as left-back. I'm just happy to be in the team."

Last season wasn't one of the most memorable in the history of the fiercely-proud Ibrox team.

They lost to arch-rivals Celtic in the League Cup Final, they were knocked out of the UEFA Cup in the Second Round by Cologne on a 6–2 aggregate and even at the halfway stage of their Premier League campaign they were FOURTEEN points behind Celtic and quoted at 100–1 to win the title!

That is most unlike Rangers who are normally in there right at the very end hunting for trophies to add to their already illustrious history.

Rangers have been rebuilding over the past two seasons. John McClelland has been part of that rebuilding. The play-anywhere star doesn't want to play anywhere but Ibrox these days, and he hopes to lead Rangers to further glory.

JOEY JONES - WELSH WONDER

If anyone ever wanted a blueprint for a footballing action man, then they should look no farther than Joey Jones, a left-back who's on the go from first whistle to last. Joey's bustling style won him admirers with Wrexham, Liverpool and Chelsea. His greatest thrill was helping Liverpool win their first European Championship – in 1977 – and his most bitter disappointment came when Wales failed to reach the 1982 World Cup Finals. It's probably too late for him to collect another European medal, but Joey still has time to inspire his country to glory.

Ricky tussles with the great West German striker Karl Heinz Rummenigge at Wembley.

TRICKY RICKY

It comes as no surprise to discover that Ricky Hill is both shy and modest. The Luton and England midfield player finds it difficult to cope when people tell him to his face that he really is one of the best young players in the League!

Much of the time Luton manager David Pleat beats everyone to the punch and gives the type of glowing reference that would set you up for life with any boss. But Hill's shyness must never be mistaken for either lack of confidence or ambition.

North London born of West Indian parents, Hill joined Luton from school and quietly set about establishing himself in the then Second Division side's squad.

He steered very clear of headlines and showed a remarkable temperament for a teenager, getting up, dusting down and continuing on with the game after even the most cynical of fouls.

It paid off. Opponents grew to respect his skills, his balance, change of place and wicked shooting power.

Hill was instrumental in a free-flowing side when Luton stormed out of Division Two as Champions with an eight-point lead in 1982. He revelled in the midfield freedom offered by Pleat's admirable loyalty to entertaining football and continued to find the net as well as creating chances for others.

But it was the appointment of Bobby Robson as England manager that granted Hill his biggest wish – to play for England.

"Obviously I had always wanted to play for England, but with so many top class players on the scene I could only hope that if I achieved a level of consistency I would get my chance.

"Some people even put me forward for the World Cup but I had a strong feeling that Ron Greenwood would not change his plans.

"Being selected for the squad was an unforgettable experience, as was winning my first cap, coming on as substitute for Tony Morley in the 2-2 European Championship draw in Denmark.

EXPERIENCE

"My first full 90-minute cap was at Wembley against World Cup Finalists West Germany. Karl Heinz Rummenigge somewhat spoiled the occasion by scoring twice to give them a 2-1 win, but the experience was priceless and I knew I had at last got my teeth into the international game.

"Now I am concerned with producing my very best form for Luton. That's what matters most, the bread and butter of the game. And if I achieve this standard I will continue to have a good chance of remaining part of the England set-up."

Gordon Strachan (left) of Aberdeen became highly-valued following his eye-catching display for Scotland against Brazil in the 1982 World Cup Finals (below).

GIVEN AWAY—NOW PRICELESS!

Gordon Strachan became one of the most sought-after players in Europe after his enthralling displays for Scotland during the World Cup Finals in Spain.

Watching the little Aberdeen maestro take on players and skip past tackles with style and grace it was easy to realise why so many managers looked on with envy.

But, amazingly, there was a day when Strachan wasn't wanted by his club!

That was back in '77 when Dundee's former manager Tommy Gemmell decided it was time for the little red-haired buzz-bomb to move on.

Gemmell, as a raiding, buccaneering full-back with that glorious Celtic side of the Sixties, rarely made mistakes.

But even he might admit he dropped a mighty clanger when he just about made a present of Strachan.

Strachan signed for a paltry £70,000 plus a player (Jim Shirra) and his career has rocketed skywards ever since.

It was Billy McNeill, Gemmell's former Parkhead colleague, who took the player to Pittodrie. McNeill is now, of course, the Celtic supremo . . . and Strachan may have been under his charge again if a deal between the Glasgow side and Dundee had gone through when Jock Stein was still boss at Celtic.

The move was actually at an advanced stage before negotiations broke down. McNeill can now only think of what-might-have-been.

For some curious reason mighty atom Gordon turns on the magic when he faces Celtic . . . even to the extent that he has twice been the target for pitch-invading fans when the Parkhead men have been in opposition!

But, so typical of Edinburgh-born Strachan, he doesn't dwell on these things. He sys: "Celtic? Yes, they're a good team. I don't purposely set out to upset their fans.

"I've got nothing against them at all. Goodness, on the afternoon of one of those attacks I actually picked up a couple of Celtic fans in my car and gave them a lift.

"I'll probably worry when the fans start to ignore me. Then I'll know I'm not doing my job properly for Aberdeen out on the pitch."

Strachan's international career really took off in Spain, but no-one in Scottish soccer was unduly surprised when he caught the imagination of just about everyone.

The player was unsettled when he returned to Pittodrie and there were stories of a transfer request, but manager Alex Ferguson was quick to say: "He's staying. He's under contract and he's not moving.

"In any case, who could afford him? The bidding would have to start at £2 million!"

The player who joined up at Dundee in '72 from Edinburgh Thistle and didn't set the heather alight at Dens Park has certainly had a change of fortune since the day Tommy Gemmell transferred him to Aberdeen.

NO SPILT MILK FOR LIVERPOOL

The Milk Cup took over from the Football League Cup in 1981-82 and is now established as a trophy every club sets its sights on winning. Yet when the competition started, in 1960-61, it was mainly ignored by the First Division clubs and unkindly called the "Mickey Mouse Cup".

For the first six years of its existence the Final was played on a home and away basis, and it was not until 1967 that the League Cup was fought for at Wembley.

The Final, between Third Division Queens Park Rangers and First Division West Bromwich Albion, turned out to be one of the most exciting ever staged, and helped to establish the competition.

Rangers won 3-2. It was no flash in the pan, for the Loftus Road side went on to take the Third Division Championship with 67 points, 12 clear of runners-up Middlesbrough.

Two years later another club from the Third, Swindon Town, captured the trophy after beating Arsenal 3-1.

That signalled the end of appearances from Third Division clubs in the Final.

REBOUND

But in 1974-75, it starred two clubs from the Second Division, Aston Villa — the very first winners of the Cup — and Norwich City. Villa won with the only goal scored, by Ray Graydon, whose penalty kick was saved by 'keeper Jim Cumbes, only for Ray to make no mistake with the rebound.

The longest running Final was staged in 1977 between Aston Villa and Everton.

The Wembley game was goalless and was replayed at Hillsborough. This time each side scored once.

The second replay, at Old Trafford, ended in a narrow 3-2 victory for Villa.

One of the most amazing upsets in the competition occurred in 1980, when unfancied Wolves stopped Nottingham Forest from completing a hat-trick of wins with an Andy Gray goal.

Liverpool, for all their success at home and in Europe, had to wait until 1981 for their first win, beating West Ham, who suffered their second Final defeat.

The following year Liverpool became first winners of the Milk Cup and retained it in 1983.

Ironically, in both Finals Liverpool recovered from being a goal down to win after extra-time!

For the second successive year Liverpool captain Graeme Souness proudly shows the Milk Cup to Reds' fans.

Peter Dodds of Champions Dundee United duels with Ian Redford of Rangers.

was another important stage for us.''

It's to be seen whether United's Championship win was a flash in the pan or whether they will remain in contention with the previous dominant forces — Celtic, Rangers and Aberdeen.

Under a manager of the calibre of Jim McLean, United stand every chance not only of remaining amongst Scotland's elite but of becoming "one of Europe's top teams", the accolade bestowed on Aberdeen by Real Madrid manager Alfredo di Stefano after his Spanish maestros' defeat in the Cup-Winners' Cup Final in Gothenburg, Sweden.

He gave full credit to The Dons. "Aberdeen finished the stronger team in atrocious conditions."

It was indeed a proud night in Aberdonian history. A convincing win for a Scottish side overdue a slice of European glory, and a tribute to the 12,000 fans who celebrated with their Spanish counterparts and won over

'Firsts' for Dundee United — and Aberdeen

One reason football continues to grip the imagination is the way it produces the most amazing twists and turns of Fate.

Dundee United, who had never before won the League Championship, either in the old First Division founded in 1890, or the present slim-line Premier Division launched in 1975, beat off the challenge of mighty Celtic, aiming for a hat-trick of titles last season.

And the crucial turning point for the Tannadice Terrors was the League match in which they beat Aberdeen,

the other surprise-packets on the Scottish scene who also achieved a unique "first" by tasting success in Europe.

United centre-half Paul Hegarty singled out his team's win over The Dons in March for special mention: "We won 2-1 at Pittodrie and it was then that I felt we were in with a big shout.

"Our 3-2 victory over Celtic in April

the local Swedes with their humour and responsible behaviour.

Just over a week later the same fans celebrated another win – in the Scottish Cup against Rangers.

Manager Alex Ferguson has assembled a side of strength and skill, a side that, with the likes of Gordon Strachan, Willie Miller, Mark McGhee, Peter Weir and John Hewitt, is destined to add further football battle honours to the banner of the Granite City's great club.

Aberdeen parade the Cup-Winners' Cup in Sweden.

51

When I relax at home pouring over the highlights of my career, my mind will often dwell on that unforgettable moment in 1975 when I was offered the captaincy of Chelsea.

"Surely not me," I thought, having been asked to lead my beloved Chelsea at the tender age of 19.

I had become the youngest player ever to captain Chelsea – and went on to lead the team for four years, relinquishing the post only when they transferred me to Manchester United in 1979.

It was memorable simply to join United, so you can imagine my delight when Dave Sexton, the manager, asked me to take over the captaincy at Old Trafford from Martin Buchan, a United stalwart for many years with tremendous leadership qualities.

I must admit, I've always enjoyed the responsibility of captaincy. I suppose it all goes back to schooldays. Some kids are leaders, others are followers.

When it came to football I never minded taking charge of things in school matches – and I'm the same today.

Funny thing is that I'd never dream of telling someone what to do or where to go *off* the field. Yet I'll talk from the start of the final whistle of a League game, bossing players around, encouraging them.

Captain of Chelsea, captain of United, could anything cap that? In a word, yes! Bobby Robson chose me to captain England against Denmark in a European Championship game in September 1982, his first match in charge, following Kevin Keegan's departure from the England scene.

But as quickly as I had risen to the

'I'M IN

Showing his leadership qualities as a lad at Stamford Bridge.

heady heights of captaining my country, my career collapsed dramatically.

I lost the captaincy of Mancheter United and England on a winter's night on the south coast in October 1982. I was stretchered off the Bournemouth pitch in a League Milk Cup-tie suffering from a fractured cheekbone. It felt bad. It was bad. It cost me the leadership of club and country.

I was out of the game for months, losing my England place and spending long anxious months wondering where my future lay.

Ray leading by example in England's draw with Denmark in 1982.

Ray admires the football intelligence of the Maine Road captain.

Ironically, shortly after I regained my fitness, injury hit Bryan Robson and I got the call to lead the United players out at Wembley for the 1983 Milk Cup Final with Liverpool.

Unfortunately, after a long, hard 120 minutes we lost 2-1. A big disappointment.

The First Division has many fine captains whose powers of leadership serve as a major inspiration to their sides. Steve Perryman takes some beating.

A one club man, Steve was the driving force behind Tottenham's two F.A. Cup Final appearances in 1981 and 1982. Who knows how much his injury problems in 1982-83 cost Spurs success in that season.

Paul Power, of Manchester City, has always been a strong leader. It doesn't surprise me that he was tempted to pull on a wig and become a lawyer rather than a footballer. He has a good brain which he manages to apply to his football at Maine Road.

One of the First Division's best captains doesn't even hold the job at his club. I'm referring to Phil Thompson. Phil has captained Liverpool and England, but Bob Paisley had no hesitation of relieving Phil of the Liverpool job when he felt Graeme Souness could offer more to the great northern club.

Souness, an excellent captain, was preferred by Liverpool at a time when Phil's career had been hampered by injury. It hurt Phil to lose the post but Liverpool's fans were not complaining

Kevin Keegan impressed me tremendously when he led England.

It was through no fault of Kevin's that England tended to struggle in those difficult times of winning a place in the 1982 World Cup Finals. His best days came at a period of decline for England, starting with Sir Alf Ramsey's latter days and accelerating alarmingly through Don Revie's reign.

Keegan and Ron Greenwood did much to restore England's morale and prestige, an era I was fortunate to experience.

CHARGE

Something I really enjoy'

SAYS RAY WILKINS

as the "machine" powered to success after success.

Two long-serving goalkeepers reckon they are pretty hot at captaincy – Ray Clemence, of Spurs, and Leicester's 'keeper Mark Wallington.

Both have led their teams into battle on occasions with notable success, Ray once having the honour of leading England against Brazil.

Peter Shilton, one of football's most dedicated professionals, is another goalkeeper to taste the glory of leading his country when Bobby Robson asked him to lead out the side against Wales in February 1983 when Bryan Robson was tied-up in a Milk Cup Semi-Final tie against Arsenal.

No disrespect to the goalkeeping brigade, but unless you've got a voice like a company sergeant-major on a barracks square, you have little or no influence over your forwards from such a withdrawn position.

Who is the best captain I've ever played under? That's a difficult one.

One of the best captains around at the moment is Bryan Robson – the man who took over from me at Manchester United and England.

As Bryan well knows, I would never begrudge him the chance he was given when I suffered that unfortunate injury at Bournemouth. I've played too much football to deny another player his chance when the man in charge has fallen by the wayside through no fault of his own.

If an opportunity presents itself in football, grab it. After all, I took Kevin Keegan's job when Bobby Robson decided to discard him from the England team.

No, there are no hard feelings when it comes to Bryan Robson's contribution to United and England. To be quite honest, he strikes me as a fine leader and I wish him every success – as he would me if the circumstances were different.

Yes, I've had my disappointments in this great game. But as I said at the start of the article, I cherish some wonderful memories of the day I was asked to "be captain".

And you can't take those away.

Kenny Dalglish shuffled nervously on those famous feet and cast anxious eyes across the vast banqueting hall of London's Cafe Royal.

Dalglish dislikes the formalities of socialising on a large scale, and it showed. Give him a red or blue shirt and a football and he will entertain thousands in a stadium with the icy calm of a man confident of his footballing ability.

But this was different. There were dozens of players he knew sitting at oval tables in a room roughly the size of three penalty boxes, but volumes of Havana smoke obscured their faces under the twinkling crystal oppulance of a dozen chandeliers and one of the game's shyest and most reserved men looked distinctly uncomfortable.

But there was no mistaking

backs as Matthews, teasing and tantalising them with his forays down the left wing. A few centre-halves had cause to remember the "Preston plumber" too, both England and Preston employing him in the number nine shirt on occasions.

An Irishman joined the elite group of men to win the elusive award twice. His name was Danny Blanchflower and his artistry at wing-half for Tottenham Hotspur and Northern Ireland earned him the trophy in 1958 and again in 1961.

The former Barnsley and Aston Villa player became one of Bill Nicholson's

first signings at White Hart Lane. Blanchflower was already a hardened international, winning his first cap for Northern Ireland in 1950.

By the time he arrived at Tottenham he was recognised as one of Britain's finest half-backs. He was never a "cruncher", preferring stealth and sophistication to unlock the tightest defences.

It came as no surprise to anyone when the Irishman was handed the award for the second time in 1961 after a momentous season at Spurs.

That was the time when the full chorus of "Glory Glory Hallelujah",

The Soccer Greats who share the honour of twice being voted Player of the Year

Four of a

Dalglish's recognition when the most famous face in football approached him.

It belonged to none other than the legendary Edson Arantes Dos Nasciemento. Pele.

The great Brazilian, recognised by most as the greatest player the game has ever seen, had made a surprise journey to Britain for the sole purpose of presenting the ace marksman of Liverpool and Scotland with one of football's most prized awards, the Football Writers' Footballer of the Year trophy.

Pele's time is precious these days. A world superstar living in retirement, he is in demand right across the globe. But when an invitation to present the award to Dalglish arrived at his home thousands of miles from English shores, he had no hesitation in grabbing his passport and making the trip.

Pele's timing was superb, for Dalglish was joining a trio of football giants who have won the Footballer of the Year award twice.

Stanley Matthews, whose sorcery with a football should have clinched membership of the Magic Circle, became the first player to receive the award in 1948 for his wing wizardry for Blackpool and England.

And long after most players would have offered their boots to a jumble sale and skipped happily into a well-earned retirement, Stan popped up again to win the award in 1963, six years after winning his 54th and last England cap and now as a Stoke City player.

Tom Finney, often just as dazzling as Matthews with a greater capacity for scoring goals, claimed the award twice in 1954 and 1957 for his efforts for Preston and England.

Finney, capped 76 times by England, had become as much a scourge of full-

(Left) Preston's Tom Finney, winner in 1954 and 1957.

54

1948, and Sir Stanley Matthews becomes the first Player of the Year.

belted in triumph by thousands of voices, could be heard all the way down Tottenham High Road, almost as far as Seven Sisters tube station.

It was the year Spurs clinched the League and Cup "double", Blanchflower, the captain, raising the trophies aloft in a never to be forgotten season.

But not since Blanchflower's eloquent speech to the Football Writers' Association and their guests in London in 1961 had any player managed to win The Footballer of the Year award twice.

It was inevitable, perhaps, that if a player was to join that illustrious group of double-award winners from football's glorious past, he would be a Liverpool player.

Glorious deeds at home in winning the Championship for a record 14th time, three triumphant European Cup campaigns, and a host of other medal-winning feats have marked Liverpool down as the most successful English club since the War.

How fitting then that their ace goal-scorer and most famous player, Kenny Dalglish, should receive his second Footballer of the Year award in 1983.

As always, Dalglish looked surprised

to be asked to receive the award from Pele.

He has little or no time for all the rigmarole associated with receiving awards, while remaining eternally grateful to those people who acknowledge the dazzling skills that have brought him close to a rare international landmark for Scotland, 100 caps.

Kenny Dalglish is the prince who prefers to remain behind his castle walls, never losing the boyish innocence that takes him to quiet corners at Anfield rather than towards the television lights.

But there he was, standing proudly before players, managers, journalists, and Pele to receive a standing ovation.

Pele's arrival was his first shock that night. But if that had rocked him on his heels, the surprise on Dalglish's face when Pele planted a kiss on his blushing left cheek left him utterly speechless.

That is the way men greet men in the sambaland of the South American continent and you don't change the habits of a lifetime when you are confronted with a hardened Scottish striker in a foreign land.

Pele, clearly relishing an opportunity to honour Britain's most respected player, spoke of the opportunities football gave for players "to love their brother players".

His mother had wanted him to be a doctor or a professor. He chose football and it had given him good fellowship, money, a reputation and so much enjoyment.

Pele froze the room by calling for a "symbolic silence" to honour those players not fortunate enough to be present at the award ceremony.

TEAM-WORK

And then it was Dalglish's turn to speak, clutching the trophy won by 33 players since its inception in 1948.

"Mr Chairman, Pele . . .' Dalglish trod a cautious speech-making path, careful to point out he was not good "at communications".

But his confidence grew, and he admitted: "I just hope I can impress upon you all how much this award means to me."

Then his Liverpool upbringing was brought into play as he went on: "Let us never forget that this is a team game. It is an award for Liverpool Football Club."

By now he had been going for two minutes and the end was in sight. His Liverpool training again flashed into view. Searching for Bob Paisley, the retiring Liverpool manager, sitting nearby, Dalglish wound-up his speech by saying: "I would like to wish the boss all that he wishes himself. I only hope that in retirement he is as successful as he has been in football."

And giving the trophy a final glance, the great Scottish striker grinned: "It's mine, I'm not sure it's deserved. But you're not getting it back."

Pele was always known as football's most modest player.

But in giving Kenny Dalglish the Footballer of the Year award the Brazilian saw the same refreshing humbleness that is rare in someone so brilliant in the world of sport.

Kenny Dalglish receives his second award from the great Pele, assisted by Jeff Powell, chairman of the Football Writers' Association. (Right) Spurs' captain Danny Blanchflower, another to do the players' coveted "double".

For over 100 years Tottenham Hotspur have been making history . . . the only non-League club to win the F.A. Cup; the first to complete the League Championship and F.A. Cup double this century . . . the first British club to win a major European trophy. Spurs have produced some of the game's

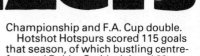

League Championship triumph in 1950-51 when they finished four points clear of Manchester United.

When ill-health forced Rowe to retire, Bill Nicholson, who joined the club as a 16-year-old £2-a-week ground-staff boy in 1936, took over.

The appointment was confirmed in October, 1958, on the morning of a home match against Everton.

The players celebrated Bill's new job with a fantastic 10-4 victory.

Three years later Tottenham became the first club this century to achieve the

Trail-blazers

finest players and thrilled millions of fans throughout the world. This is their story . . .

Tottenham Hotspur have blazed more trails than any other club in British soccer history.

In 1901 they defeated Sheffield United to become the first non-League club to win the F.A. Cup, after taking the revolutionary step of appointing a player-manager, James Cameron from Everton.

Seven years later Spurs applied to join the Football League, but were rejected!

Then the Southern League refused to accept them back and the club faced extinction.

Fortunately, Stoke City resigned from the League and Spurs were elected by one vote over Lincoln. They showed their appreciation by winning immediate promotion from the Second Division.

But real success didn't come until 1919-20 when they won the Second Division Championship with 70 points.

The following season, Spurs finished sixth in the First Division and scored 17 goals in their march to the F.A. Cup Final at Stamford Bridge.

In torrential rain Spurs beat Wolves thanks to a Jimmy Dimmock goal. The Cup was presented for the first time by a reigning monarch, King George V.

In the 1932-33 season Spurs crowned their Golden Jubilee year by winning promotion after five seasons in the Second Division.

Tottenham's high-speed, along-the-ground football earned them the nickname The Greyhounds.

After the war Arthur Rowe's push-and-run style was to stimulate English football. It was enormously successful and took Spurs to their first ever

Championship and F.A. Cup double.

Hotshot Hotspurs scored 115 goals that season, of which bustling centre-forward Bobby Smith claimed 33.

After beating Burnley 3-0 in the F.A. Cup Semi-Finals, Spurs faced Leicester City at Wembley and goals from Bobby Smith and Terry Dyson gave them a 2-0 win.

Tottenham retained the F.A. Cup in 1962, beating Burnley 3-1 with goals from Jimmy Greaves, Bobby Smith and Danny Blanchflower (penalty).

Success at Wembley put Tottenham in the European Cup-Winners' Cup the following season. They beat holders Atletico Madrid 5-1 in Rotterdam.

So Super Spurs became the first British club to win a major European competition.

In January, 1967, Spurs embarked on a tremendous run of 24 games without defeat which included a 2-1 victory over Chelsea in the first all-London F.A. Cup Final at Wembley.

Tottenham's next triumph was their

The first "double" winners of this century parade the F.A. Cup.

first Football League Cup Final win in 1970-71 when the beat Third Division Aston Villa with two goals from Martin Chivers.

The following season was the first for the U.E.F.A. Cup competition (formerly the Fairs Cup) and Spurs' unexpected opponents in the Final were Wolves, the first time two English clubs had met in a European Final.

Spurs won 3-2 on aggregate to become the first British club to capture two European trophies.

Tottenham won the League Cup goal. So the scene was set for a Wembley replay – the first ever.

With the score 2-2, Tottenham's dramatic winner by Ricky Villa has been described as the best seen at Wembley.

In 1981-82 Spurs reached the League Cup Final (renamed the Milk Cup) and F.A. Cup Final to become the first club to play in two domestic Finals in the same season.

Liverpool won the Milk Cup, while the F.A. Cup Final against Queens Park Rangers needed a replay for the second year in succession.

Fighting Rangers were beaten by a Glenn Hoddle penalty and the trophy returned to White Hart Lane.

An amazing feature of Tottenham's glory has often been the figure 1 in the date.

They have achieved success in 1901 (F.A. Cup), 1921 (F.A. Cup), 1951 (Champions), 1961 (double), 1971 (League Cup) and 1981 (F.A. Cup).

With so much talent at White Hart Lane it's a safe bet Spurs fans won't have to wait until 1991 for success.

Tottenham

again in 1972-73 with a goal from substitute Ralph Coates, but in 1974 failed to win their fourth trophy in four seasons when they lost to Feyenoord in the U.E.F.A. Cup Final.

The great Bill Nicholson resigned soon after. Former Arsenal star Terry Neill took over on Friday, 13th September, 1974, and was dogged by bad luck until the last six games of the season when Spurs rallied to beat relegation by one point.

Neill returned to Arsenal at the end of the following 1975-76 season and was replaced by his coach Keith Burkinshaw.

Failure to sign big name players was not due to any lack of effort on Burkinshaw's part.

A brave decision was needed and the Spurs boss made it in July, 1978, by signing Argentinians Ricardo Villa and Osvaldo Ardiles.

The World Cup winning duo were to be the foundations for the new Spurs of the Eighties.

In 1980-81, Tottenham, inspired by the South American stars, reached the F.A. Cup Final.

Tommy Hutchison put Manchester City ahead, but Spurs equalised when the same player put through his own

THE BEGINNING

In 1882 a group of youngsters gathered under a lamp-post in Tottenham High Road to form a club that took the name Hotspur from the Duke of Northumberland whose family owned much of the neighbouring land.

Tottenham's first ground was behind the Northumberland Arms public house and they used an old railway wagon as a grandstand. The club took 85p in receipts from their first match.

In 1895 the club went professional, paying their players between 75p and £1.25p a week.

Three years later Spurs moved to their present site of White Hart Lane.

THE HOTSPURS

Many of the game's greatest players have worn the famous white shirt of Tottenham Hotspur.

One of the best-known and certainly most successful was DANNY BLANCHFLOWER, captain of that great 1961 Double side.

He began his career with Barnsley in 1949 before moving to Aston Villa.

In December, 1954, Arthur Rowe persuaded the Northern Ireland international to join Spurs for £30,000 instead of Arsenal.

Alongside Danny, twice voted Footballer of the Year, in so many triumphs was barrel-chested DAVE MACKAY, bought by Bill Nicholson from Hearts.

Spurs were building for the future, just as James Cameron had done in the 1900's with well-known players of the time, SANDY BROWN, DAVID COPELAND and SANDY TAIT.

The hero of Tottenham's Cup victory in 1901 was Brown who scored in every Round with a total of 15.

In the 1920's came JIMMY SEED, an inside-forward who had been badly gassed in the First World War and discarded by Sunderland.

He arrived at the same time as JIMMY DIMMOCK, a free-scoring left-winger who went to play for England alongside Seed.

Tottenham's first League success came in 1950-51 with ARTHUR ROWE'S (a centre-half who made over 200 League appearances for the club), push-and-run style.

Their flowing football established players such as ALF RAMSEY, a full-back bought from Southampton for £21,000, RON BURGESS, arguably the finest wing-half Spurs ever produced, EDDIE BAILEY, who controlled the midfield, TED DITCHBURN, a brilliant and spectacular goalkeeper and BILL NICHOLSON, a tough and uncompromising wing-half.

Ten years later when Spurs won the Double it was led by manager Nicholson and captain Blanchflower.

Nicholson's Double side was one of the greatest Britain has ever seen . . . Scotland 'keeper BILL BROWN, defenders PETER BAKER and RON HENRY, centre-half MAURICE NORMAN, centre-forward BOBBY SMITH, wingers CLIFF JONES and TERRY DYSON, inside-forwards LES ALLEN and JOHN WHITE, so tragically killed by lightning

Ricky Villa scores from an incredible solo effort to win the Cup in the Wembley replay in 1981.

on a golf course, and JIMMY GREAVES, signed in December, 1961, from AC Milan.

The England international went on to become the club's record goalscorer with 37 in 1962-63 and an overall total of 220 between 1961 and 1970.

In June, 1964, Nicholson signed a relatively unknown goalkeeper PAT JENNINGS from Watford after just 48 League games.

But the Northern Ireland international was to prove one of the biggest bargains of all-time at £30,000.

Jennings helped Spurs to F.A. Cup success in 1967. In that side were TERRY VENABLES, CRYIL KNOWLES, MIKE ENGLAND, ALAN GILZEAN and ALAN MULLERY.

The early Seventies established STEVE PERRYMAN, who joined the club from school in 1967 and has already given sterling service.

In March, 1970, Nicholson caused a sensation by setting a new British transfer record fee when he signed MARTIN PETERS one of England's 1966 World Cup winning stars, from West Ham for £200,000 plus Jimmy Greaves.

Although Spurs won the League and U.E.F.A. Cups in the early Seventies it wasn't until Keith Burkinshaw took over from Terry Neill and pulled off that remarkable Ardiles and Villa double deal that Tottenham looked like returning to their halcyon days.

Before the 1980-81 season Burkinshaw signed strikers GARTH CROOKS from Stoke City and STEVE ARCHIBALD from Aberdeen, for a club record fee of £800,000.

They formed the most lethal striking partnership in the First Division which owed much to the searching passes of GLENN HODDLE.

After winning the F.A. Cup in 1981, Burkinshaw signed England 'keeper RAY CLEMENCE from Liverpool, and Mr. Versatile himself, GARY MABBUTT from Bristol Rovers.

With the emergence of youngsters such as MIKE HAZARD, TERRY GIBSON, GARRY BROOKE, MARK FALCO, GARY O'REILLY, ALISTAIR DICK and GRAHAM ROBERTS, Tottenham can look forward to many more trail-blazing years.

A golden boot for a golden boy! Superstar Kevin Keegan proudly hugs his glittering prize.

another hero from The Dell – Ron Davies in 1966-67.

Only one man with the golden goal-touch over the past two decades has succeeded in getting four hat-tricks – in 1962-63 and 1963-64 – and that's Jimmy Greaves, who while with Spurs was in the chart more times than anyone else.

He also got "three three's" – in 1968-69.

The only other Spurs top scorer was Steve Archibald, who shared the award.

Last season's SHOOT/Adidas award winner, Watford's Luther Blissett, scored one hat-trick, in his club's 5-3 defeat of Notts County, and four goals in one game – against Sunderland.

Luther ended up with a goals tally of 27, the highest for five seasons, and is hoping to improve this time around when his club aim to finish one place higher – in the Championship spot.

But Luther has some serious challengers in Ian Rush, who was hampered by a groin injury at the final stage of last season; Spurs' Alan Brazil; John Wark of Ipswich and John Deehan of fellow East Anglians Norwich.

Luther Blissett (right) after scoring his first-ever hat-trick in League football – against Sunderland in September, 1982.

MASTER MARKSMEN

Quiz question: In the past twenty seasons two clubs have provided the First Division's top scorer four times, yet neither have won the Championship. One is Tottenham Hotspur. Name the other!

Unless you're a fan of the particular club, or have already sneaked a look at the column of master marksman, it's odds on you won't even guess the answer.

It's Southampton, the coastal club whose highest-ever finishing position in the First Division came in 1980-81 when they became sixth in the table.

Their most recent player to top the scoring stakes was Kevin Keegan, with 26 goals that earned him the SHOOT/Adidas award in 1981-82.

Amazingly enough, Kevin failed to collect a single hat-trick.

The previous Saints winner, Phil Boyer, scored three goals less than Kevin, yet managed to include a hat-trick of hat-tricks!

This feat was also achieved by

Tops over Twenty years

Season	Player	Club	Goals
1963-64	Jimmy Greaves	Tottenham Hotspur	35
1964-65	Jimmy Greaves	Tottenham Hotspur	29
	Andy McEvoy	Blackburn Rovers	29
1965-66	Roger Hunt	Liverpool	30
1966-67	Ron Davies	Southampton	37
1967-68	George Best	Manchester United	28
	Ron Davies	Southampton	28
1968-69	Jimmy Greaves	Tottenham Hotspur	27
1969-70	Jeff Astle	WBA	25
1970-71	Tony Brown	WBA	28
1971-72	Francis Lee	Manchester City	33
1972-73	Bryan Robson	West Ham United	28
1973-74	Mick Channon	Southampton	21
1974-75	Malcolm Macdonald	Newcastle United	21
1975-76	Ted MacDougall	Norwich City	23
1976-77	Malcolm Macdonald	Arsenal	25
	Andy Gray	Aston Villa	25
1977-78	Bob Latchford	Everton	30
1978-79	Frank Worthington	Bolton Wanderers	24
1979-80	Phil Boyer	Southampton	23
1980-81	Steve Archibald	Tottenham Hotspur	20
	Peter Withe	Aston Villa	20
1981-82	Kevin Keegan	Southampton	26
1982-83	Luther Blissett	Watford	27

"We've won the Cup!" A marvellous night for the Red Devils.

CAN UNITED HIT SIX?

If the prediction of Manchester United manager Ron Atkinson comes true, then the side he has built is all set to add to the F.A. Cup they won in that thrilling replay against Brighton last May.

"Once we overcome the hurdle of winning our first trophy, then others will soon follow," big Ron had said.

United turned on a wonder show in that Thursday night replay against a Seagulls' side that had held them to a 2-2 draw the previous Saturday, and had come within an ace of winning the trophy but for a courageous save by 'keeper Gary Bailey.

Two goals from captain Bryan Robson, and one each from Norman Whiteside and Arnold Muhren (a penalty conversion), saw United win by the widest margin since the Final was first staged at Wembley, 'way back in 1923.

It was the Old Trafford team's fifth Final win. The first was in 1909, when they beat Bristol City 1-0; the second in 1948 against Blackpool with a 4-2 scoreline; the third by 3-1 versus Leicester City and the fourth in 1977 when they robbed Champions Liverpool of the "double" by beating them 2-1.

The 1983 triumph was a wonderful birthday present for United director Sir Matt Busby, giving him an extra reason for celebrating reaching the age of 74 after a glorious career.

It was Sir Matt who laid the foundations for United's most successful era – in the Sixties, crowned by a European Cup Win in 1968 when they beat Portuguese Champions Benfica by a resounding 4-1 after extra-time at Wembley.

Since then trophies have been few and far between. But the rampaging Red Devils have given due warning they are in with more than a fighting chance of becoming the team of the Eighties!

United's Ray Wilkins duels with Brighton's Gary Howlett in the replay. Ray failed to score then, but his goal in the Final proper ranks as one of Wembley's best-ever.

Forest memory fires Frankie

Nottingham Forest's John Robertson converts the penalty-kick that brought Frank Gray his European Cup medal. It has inspired him to seek another distinguished honour . . .

As the only British player to appear in European Cup Finals for two different clubs, Frank Gray already carries a considerable burden of fame.

Leeds United's exciting Scottish international left-back has already achieved a list of career highlights that would do credit to a top class professional on the verge of retirement.

Yet he believes that all his ambitions are still ahead of him!

"I want a League Championship medal," said Gray: "to go with the one my brother Eddie won with Leeds. And I want to be a winner with Scotland after coming so close in the past.

"I want an F.A. Cup winner's medal as well. So, as you can see, it's all there for me to achieve."

Glasgow-born Gray, in his second spell with Leeds, joined the club from school when Eddie was still a dazzling left-winger. He soon established himself in the first team and was a member of the United side beaten so controversially by Bayern Munich in the 1975 European Cup Final in Paris.

"That was a terrible night. Our supporters went wild and got into all sorts of trouble. And we really felt sick about a disallowed goal and a penalty we believed we should have been awarded."

But Gray's future, it seemed, lay elsewhere. He was signed by Brian Clough after 193 League games and 17 goals for United and soon after played in the 1980 League Cup Final at Wembley.

"I finished up a loser again," he said: "We didn't touch our best form and Wolves sneaked a scrappy affair by 1-0."

But Forest were already reigning European Champions and Gray was an important member of their side when they recaptured the trophy at the end of that season.

"John Robertson scored a cracking first-half goal that shattered Hamburg and Peter Shilton was world class in goal as, led by Kevin Keegan, they threw everything at us. But at last I had my winners' medal."

It came as a shock to Forest fans when Clough agreed to let Gray rejoin his brother, by then manager, at Elland Road in the summer of 1981. "It was a bit of a wrench because I had a good time at Forest. But Leeds were my first club and I was delighted to take up the challenge of trying to re-establish them as a force again.

"I was around when the great side was sweeping everything before it. I know what the place is like during such a period and I want to collect those medals wearing a white shirt."

Super Focus ARTHUR ALBISTON MAN UTD

Height: 5 ft 7½ ins

Weight: 10st 10lbs

Nickname: Chips

Birthday: 14-7-57

Birthplace: Edinburgh.

First club: School Team

Biggest disappointment: Not having a league div 1 medal

Most memorable match for (country): Only one, v N. Ireland.

Most memorable match at club level: F.A. Cup Final v Liverpool

Superstition: None

Person who has helped me most in my career: My Father

Favourite TV show: Any sports programme

Favourite food: Italian

Favourite drink: Tea

Favourite other sports: Tennis, Golf

Car I'd like to have: None in Particular.

Present car: Renault 18

Which person in the world would you most like to meet? Lee Trevino

Most treasured football memento: Scotland Shirt

My best friend in football: My 10 team-mates.

Autograph: *Arthur Albiston*

He made his Scotland debut against Northern Ireland in Belfast.

Arthur would like a chat with his golfing idol Lee Trevino.

Arthur (second from left at the back) selects as his most memorable match the 1977 F.A. Cup Final v. Liverpool. United won 2-1.

Should Liverpool once again win the League title this season, it's inconceivable that any other team will be able to match their record of Championship successes this century.

Thanks to an amazing 20-year domination in which time they've captured the title nine times, Liverpool's 14 Championships means they're six wins ahead of nearest rivals Arsenal.

And with no sign of Liverpool's reign coming to an end, it's difficult to envisage that gap closing much in the immediate future.

The relentless turnover of talent at Anfield means that The Reds never come to the end of an era, unlike recent Champions Leeds and Derby who are now in the Second Division.

And it's only after 16 years that even Manchester United are beginning to show signs of a serious challenge for Liverpool's crown.

In recent seasons, United have been able to boast the soundest defence in the First Division. Yet until the emergence of the Frank Stapleton and Norman Whiteside partnership they never had the attack to match.

But with the multi-million pound squad assembled by manager Ron Atkinson, United now possess the kind of strength in depth which Liverpool have always known is essential for the 42-match slog of a League campaign.

Despite Arsenal having top names in their side, including Charlie Nicholas, it's not easy to see them adding to their tally of eight Championships.

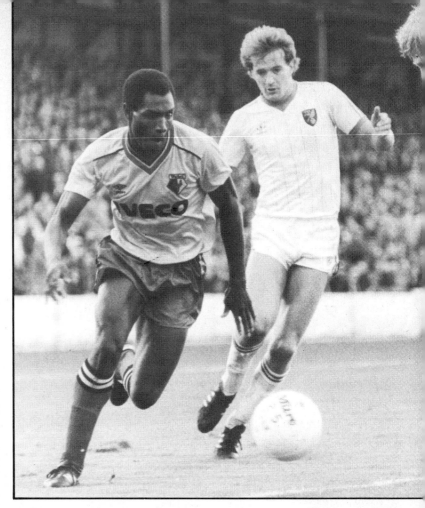

THE GREAT TITLE RACE...

Considering that five of those successes came during the 1930's and ony one has been in the last 30 years, it's about time The Gunners gave their fans something more to boast about than an unbroken membership in the First Division dating back to 1919.

Another team with a proud record in the League Championship stakes are Aston Villa, who, like Manchester United, have exactly half as many titles to their credit as Liverpool.

Villa are the only team who've managed to interrupt Liverpool's recent domination, their 1981 success sandwiched on either side by two Liverpool triumphs.

They failed to recapture that Championship form the following season, but last term Tony Barton's team showed signs that they will be there or thereabouts once again in the final reckoning.

The only team with any real number of title successes likely to bother Liverpool are their Merseyside rivals

The Blues from Maine Road are out to gain one of the three promotion spots. Here, former City striker David Cross heads an equaliser last season against Spurs.

SECOND DIVISION
Man.City good enoug
to bounce back?

League on only two occasions, in 1951 and 1961. Despite all their star names, it's hard to see Spurs ever quite managing to capture the consistency essential for a title victory.

Ipswich tasted Championship glory at the first attempt in 1962, but they haven't managed to repeat that feat despite a number of near misses under former boss Bobby Robson.

Sunderland, who have actually captured the League title on six occasions, have now gone 48 years without adding title number seven. Considering their apparent penchant for gambling with relegation, it's hard to see them doing much to alter that situation just yet.

Promoted Wolves, who spend much of their time travelling between the First and Second Divisions, have won the League three times while Midland rivals West Bromwich Albion and Nottingham Forest have one title each.

Exactly half of this season's First Division have never managed to win the Championship. Of those eleven clubs bidding for their first success, Southampton and Watford would appear to have the best chances of achieving that aim.

Southampton, after a slow start last season, gradually picked up and by the end of the term the young team assembled by Lawrie McMenemy was showing signs of real quality.

Watford finished their first season in Division One in runners-up spot, a notable achievement by anybody's standards.

have contained so many big names from football history.

One team who'll be looking for immediate promotion are Manchester City, who have already won the Second Division a record six times.

The former millionaire club have fallen on desperately hard times recently, but they still have enough class players to be pushing very hard for the title.

Sheffield Wednesday, who've won the Second Division five times before, will also be well to the fore, as will other previous Division Two Champions Derby, Newcastle and perhaps Middlesbrough.

Another fallen giant looking to get back to the First Division are Portsmouth, who became the first club to win the Third Division for the second time last season.

FIRST DIVISION
Can Watford go one-better?

FOURTH DIVISION
York's first Championship?

Fourth Division York ('keeper Roger Jones in action above) hope to win their first title. (Left) Sheffield United's Keith Edwards, about to score, could help his club achieve a "football first".

THIRD DIVISION
Sheffield Utd for a unique foursome?

at Goodison Park, Everton.

In recent seasons they have finished strongly to consistently end up in the top half of the table, but it's unlikely that they'll be adding to their seven Championships for a few years yet.

Of the other big names in the First Division, it's quite surprising how rarely they've succeeded in what is generally regarded as the toughest League in the world.

Spurs, for all their marvellous tradition in the F.A. Cup, have won the

If they can avoid the fate of a Swansea side who struggled and were eventually relegated in their second season at the top, we can see no reason why Graham Taylor's forthright young side shouldn't build on last season's encouraging start.

West Ham, despite a reputation for fine football, have never finished higher than sixth place, and neither have Coventry City despite 17 successive seasons in the top flight.

Newly-promoted QPR and Leicester will do magnificently to even match their previous best places of runners-up, but Norwich must have a very good chance of improving on their best-ever tenth place if they can reproduce the form which sent them shooting up the table at the tail-end of last season.

The Second Division can seldom

Hull, Oxford, Burnley and Rotherham will be out to emulate Pompey's feat this season.

No club has ever won the First, Second, Third and Fourth Division Championships, but Sheffield United have a chance to do just that this season.

One team who *have* won four different Championships are Grimsby Town, who have captured the Second, Third, Third (North) and Fourth Division titles.

But spare a thought for 13 of the Football League 92 clubs who have never won the right to call themselves Champions.

They are Aldershot, Bournemouth, Chester, Colchester, Crewe, Exeter, Halifax, Hartlepool, Rochdale, Swindon, Torquay, Wigan and York.

Iain McCulloch hasn't forgotten the days when playing football took second place to his job as a heating engineer.

And Notts County's star striker believes the eight years he spent in the "outside world" provided his incentive to become a top-class footballer.

McCulloch was 23 when he made his £80,000 move from Kilmarnock to Meadow Lane five years ago – and that left him with some catching up to do.

He recalled: "It was a difficult period for me because I had to get used to a new way of life in every sense.

"Inevitably it took time for me to settle in England but the biggest difference was being able to concentrate my full attention on playing football.

"While I was at Kilmarnock, is was a case of dashing home from work and then, a couple of nights a week, going straight out again for training.

"And on countless occasions, I was busy fitting someone's heating system on a Saturday morning – then off to

in a full international.

"I like to think of myself as a late-developer and I'm sure in my own mind that my game has improved 10 per cent every year since I moved down from Scotland.

"Obviously there must come a time when I will stop imroving, but I reckon it will take me another couple of years to reach my peak.

"When I joined Notts County, I felt I had the ability to make the grade in the full-time game but like most of our players, I wasn't sure about going into the First Division.

"That changed, though, in our first game after winning promotion when we went to Villa Park and won.

"Villa were the League Champions at the time and I remember thinking during the course of that game that their players were no better than me.

"The same thing happened with the other lads and although the media and the public in general have been reluctant to take us seriously, we have proved we can hold our own alongside the best in the country."

'HOW 'LATE STARTER' IAIN MADE THE GRADE....

play in a game in the afternoon.

"Naturally I've asked myself many times whether I would have been a better player had I been discovered as a 16-year-old and gone through the normal apprenticeship.

"But I reckon it was knowing the price of failure that made me so determined to make the grade with Notts County.

"I'm not saying that footballers have an easy life because they don't. It is a pleasant way of earning a living, though, and maybe I'm more aware of that than most."

It has been a hard struggle for Notts to get themselves accepted as a club worthy of a place among the giants of

English football. Their unfair image has been a handicap to the ambitious McCulloch.

But the determined Scot has overcome that disadvantage to establish a reputation as one of the most feared strikers in the country . . . and his international ambitions remain intact.

McCulloch claimed a place in Jock Stein's original squad of 40 for the World Cup in Spain and although he was eventually left behind, that didn't worry him too much.

He said: "The important thing at that stage was that I figured in the manager's thoughts and although I've had a couple of games for the Scotland Under-21 side, I just hope I get a chance

At the start of last season young Dundee goalkeeper Colin Kelly had no thoughts of first team football.

He was third-choice at Dens Park behind Scottish Under-21 star Bobby Geddes and the experienced Andy Blair. Inside two months Kelly, once rejected by Hibs, was in the top side . . . and there was no looking back.

"It was a fabulous experience," he says. "I was hoping to get into the team, of course, but I thought I would have to wait quite a bit longer.

"In fact, I was happy to be at Dens Park, at all. I was on the scrapheap when Hibs told me I wasn't good enough.

"On the day I first joined up, Eddie Turnbull, the manager who had signed me, was leaving the club. I was going in one door as he was going out the other.

"Willie Ormond then took over and gave me a few first team games, but when he quit and Berti Auld took over it was quite obvious my face didn't quite fit.

"When I was eventually freed I was out of the game for a spell until I decided to try my luck with Dundee.

"They very kindly offered me a couple of trials and, thankfully, things

Dundee's Colin Kelly

went well for me and manager Donald Mackay offered me a contract which I couldn't sign quickly enough."

Mackay thinks very highly of the youngster and has already gone on record as saying he should be capped at Under-21 level by Scotland.

"But if Scotland want him they'll have to move fast," warned the Dundee boss at the time. "England could cap him because he was born in London.

"However, he can play for Scotland because his parents are Scottish."

Kelly, then, could be following in the steps of Bob Wilson and David Harvey, two Englishmen who kept goal for Scotland despite being born on the other side of the Border.

"It's a nice thought," admits Kelly, "but I'm just quite happy to try to hold down a first team place at Dens Park.

"I'll take things as they come. Football is a totally unpredictable game . . . you never know what is just around the corner."

Donald Mackay should know a good goalkeeper when he sees one . . . he was a more than capable custodian with Dundee's city rivals United.

"If Colin's even half as good as me, he'll be doing okay," jokes the Dundee manager.

From scrapheap to stardom

Although born in London, Colin has Scottish parents and is eligible to play for Scotland. In that event, he would be following Bob Wilson — now a TV presenter — shown guarding Arsenal's goal against Leeds United in 1973.

West Ham's Paul Goddard and his wife take a back seat to their pet Great Dane.

Away from football, Man United's Gary Bailey keeps mentally sharp with the use of a computer.

OFF T

Ipswich's John Wark with the puppets given to him by team-mate Frans Thijssen's wife.

Man. City's Paul Power enjoys nothing better than to relax with his family.

Spurs' Mike Hazard moves even faster off the field — thanks to his high-powered sports saloon.

Arsenal's Kenny Sansom relives magic moments with his personal scrapbook.

Dundee United's Paul Sturrock enjoys pulling a pint and talking football at "Luggy's", the pub he runs.

Football's a team game, but Man. United's Bryan Robson believes in "do it yourself" when his home needs decorating.

E PARK

Smile, please! Man. United's Arthur Albiston operates a camera for a change.

"Old Boy" Luther Blissett of Watford visits his former school in North London.

t Brom's Cyrille Regis raises ks with his electrifying lays. But not when working at ther trade. He's a qualified trician.

Joe Corrigan monopolised Man. City's goal. But he'll share the game "Monopoly" with his family!

Footballers are BORN not MADE

You must have heard the saying "Footballers are born not made." Training and coaching helps, but it is rare for anyone to make the grade without a natural aptitude for the game that had not shown itself when they were at primary school.

Take the case of one of the most talented of post-war footballers, George Best. His family have a photograph of young George kicking a ball before he was two years old. When he played the game as a kid in Belfast he was already a football fanatic and even dribbled a ball all the way to school and back each day. No wonder he became such an expert at the art of dribbling.

To begin with scouts disregarded George because he was too small, but his lack of stature was ignored by Manchester United's Northern Ireland scout, Bob Bishop, and when George Best signed for the Old Trafford club they sent the Cregagh Boys Club a donation of £150.

Another boy who used to kick a tennis ball all the way to school and back is Trevor Brooking who developed into one of the country's finest two-footed players. His Dad played centre-half for a Metropolitan Police team and encouraged both Trevor and elder brother Tony to become two-footed players from the age of four or five when they used to practise regularly in the garden.

Natural two-footed players are not as numerous as one might think. Indeed, it is painful to watch even some international stars working the ball onto their right foot before trying a shot. Trevor's Dad obviously felt that wasn't good enough for a top class professional and West Ham United have reaped the benefit of Trevor Brooking's skill in well over 500 matches. Just think, he was the youngest player in his school side at the age of eight and saw his first West Ham game when he was only 10. There was never any doubt which club Trevor Brooking was going to play for although others showed an interest in him.

There's nothing like dribbling a tennis ball to develop skill and most of the greatest players began in this way, but one of the finest of them all was so poor that he couldn't even afford such a luxury and played his earliest football with a man's sock stuffed with rags and newspapers. This was Pelé who made his first money as a shoeshine boy. Pelé, however, was another natural who had the encouragement of his father and football was in his blood. Dad was a professional and Pelé's uncle had also played the game. Indeed, Dad continued to play even after a serious knee injury made every game a painful one. But he played because he needed the money. How different for young Pelé once he had become a world star.

Being brought up in a football-loving atmosphere appears to help. England's greatest international, Bobby Moore, was taken to football matches by his parents when still a babe in arms, for his Dad was an official of Barking Town's supporters club and travelled with the team wherever they played. Bobby played his earliest football in the streets and for Barking Primary School. Indeed, the man who captained England in 90 of his 108 games first captained his school team at the age of 10.

Lou Macari's Dad was also a football fanatic who played for Leytonstone, and Lou was soaking up the soccer atmosphere from the age of two when he became Leytonstone's mascot and used to trot out with the team. Those who have heard Lou Macari's Scottish accent may wonder about this early London football influence, but although born in Scotland Lou lived in London from the age of six months until returning North of the Border at about the age of 10.

WON THE LOT

There he began playing for his school team near Largs and it was a team that won everything in sight while Lou developed a burning desire to join Celtic. Indeed, he became a keen Celtic supporter and travelled many miles to watch them play both at home and away. He achieved his ambition when they signed him at the age of 14.

When Kevin Keegan was playing in his little back garden in Doncaster his hero was Billy Wright of Wolves and England. Today Kevin is one of the richest men in British football but he was born in a Doncaster slum area, since built over in a modern town centre development. When he wasn't kicking a ball around his back garden he played in Doncaster's Hyde Park. His uncle bought him his first football and young Kevin made his first money by selling firewood and washing cars. He even admits to getting into Doncaster Rovers games without paying, a little matter of being poor wasn't going to keep him away from his beloved football and he first appeared for his school team as goalkeeper.

Brazil's Pele shows his brilliance by shooting past the Czech 'keeper in a 1970 World Cup Finals game in which the eventual overall winners triumphed 4-1.

heart when they made that mistake.

Alan Ball, however, was destined to become a footballer as soon as he was born, for his Dad was a professional and young Alan used to go to watch him play from about the age of four. Allan Ball senior appeared in the League with Southport, Oldham and Rochdale, and almost as soon as young Alan could walk he set about encouraging him to play football. More than that, because as Alan got older, it was obvious that he lacked weight, Dad set about making him one of the fittest boys around.

Alan Ball possessed a natural determination that came through on the football field and although he was the smallest boy in his village school team at Farnworth, Bolton, he had that valuable will to win.

Talk about being thrown in at the deep end. Alan Ball went straight into Blackpool's League side for the opening game of his first season as a professional with them. It was against Liverpool before a 56,000 crowd at Anfield, and Blackpool won 2-1. Obviously Blackpool never doubted the ability of a 17-year-old who had been groomed for stardom by his Dad.

Rangers star, Derek Johnstone, is another player who didn't have much to learn after signing for the Blues. In fact it was only two months after signing for them at the age of 16 in 1970 that he played his first game in the League against Cowdenbeath and scored two of his side's four goals. Only a week later he appeared in the League Cup Final against Celtic and scored the winner before a crowd of over 106,000.

What a way to begin an illustrious career. Derek was already a well built lad when he was at Primary School and was the youngest boy in the school team. From an early age he lived and breathed football, nothing else mattered, and he was soon scoring goals galore. No doubt he often dreamt of scoring the winner for Rangers against Celtic, but even he could not have realised that he would achieve this in a Cup Final before his 17th birthday.

George Best – probably the most talented player to be produced in the British Isles. (Below): Alan Ball followed in his late father's footsteps.

At the age of 14 Kevin Keegan was turned down by Coventry City because they thought he was too small! They are not the only club to have missed a star in such a way. Scunthorpe United discovered him playing in Sunday League soccer and we all know what happened after that.

Another player who suffered the indignity of being discarded because he was too small, but was packed with so much talent that there was no way such a rebuff would stop him from reaching the top was Alan Ball, former star of Blackpool, Everton, Arsenal, Southampton, England and Bristol Rovers. Bolton Wanderers was the club who might have broken this boy's

JIMMY CASE-BRIGHTON BLOCK-BUSTER

It was a mighty shot from Jimmy that knocked out his former club Liverpool in last season's F.A. Cup Fifth Round, and set The Seagulls on their best-ever run in the competition.

Mac the knife

TWISTING and turning like an eel, Frank McGarvey cuts through the back-tracking rear-guard as a knife would slice through butter.

Not surprisingly the Celtic striker is known as "Mac The Knife" when he gets into his stride and heads straight for the jugular vein of the opposition.

But he was Mac The Strife a few years ago as he admits: "My confidence drained completely during my spell with Liverpool before returning North of the Border. The nearest I came to a first team game at Anfield was a place on the substitutes' bench.

"It didn't matter how many goals I scored for the reserves — and I netted a few — I realised I wasn't going to get an easy passage into the top side."

CONFIDENCE

Eventually McGarvey, after signing for £300,000 from St. Mirren, decided his future lay in Scotland and he was delighted to join his boyhood idols Celtic in a swift £275,000 deal.

"I reckon it took me about two years to completely restore my confidence," says McGarvey. "and, as everyone knows, confidence is absolutely crucial to a player in my position."

McGarvey is now a firm favourite with the Celtic fans and manager Billy McNeill underlines: "His attitude is first class. He's always in there looking for the ball, helping his team-mates, putting pressure on defenders and having a shot at goal. What more can you ask of a striker?"

ROSSI AND

what makes them extra-special?

Paolo Rossi and Karl-Heinz Rummenigge. They're both prodigious goalscorers. They're both European Footballers of the Year. And they're both world-wide superstars.

Why? What makes them extra-special? What have they got in common? What have they got that thousands of other strikers haven't?

"Kalle" Rummenigge and "Bambino di Oro" Rossi were brought face-to-face in the 1982 World Cup Final. But,

thanks to the West German's injury, it was no fair contest. Rossi notched his sixth goal of the tournament in Italy's surge to triumph, and a few months later he grabbed the European Footballer of the Year Award which Rummenigge had inherited from Kevin Keegan and retained for two years.

Their birthdays are just two days apart, and astrologers might claim that the stars had something to do with their similar superstar stories. Yet Karl-Heinz's birth date (September 25th 1955) puts him under the Libra sign, while Rossi's September 23rd 1956 makes the "Bambino" a Virgo.

Both played their first competitive football in their local teams. Karl-Heinz with Borussia Lippstadt, and Paolo with Prato and Cattolica. Both were then lucky enough to serve apprenticeships in great teams packed with star names. Karl-Heinz, signed by Bayern Munich for £12,000 in 1974, found himself struggling for a place in a side that contained Beckenbauer, Maier, Hoeness and Muller and was dominating European club football. 16-year-old Paolo arrived at Juventus in time to admire schoolboy idols Altafini, Anastasi, Bettega, Causio and Zoff. What they learned in these formative years undoubtedly made a profound impression on their development as footballers.

But from that moment, their careers could hardly have been more different. While Rummenigge's route to the top was a case of steady progression and loyalty to Bayern Munich, Rossi was being shunted around Italy like a goods wagon.

At Juventus he had the bad luck to

break a wrist and to need three cartilage operations – which convinced the Turin club that Rossi was too frail to make the grade as a striker in Italy's tough First Division. Off he went on loan to Como, where he only made the first team six times in the whole of the 1975-76 season. Then came a move downwards to Second Division Lanerossi in the northern town of Vicenza.

Suddenly, the superstar Rossi emerged. His 21 goals lifted Lanerossi into the First Division, and in the 1977-78 season he topped the goal charts with 24 from 30 games. Lanerossi hit the dizzy heights of European football, and Paolo, having made just two international appearances against Belgium and Spain, suddenly found himself first-choice striker in the Italy team that did so well in the 1978 World Cup in Argentina.

But disaster was just around the corner. Despite Rossi's 15 goals, Lanerossi were relegated in 1979 and Paolo was shunted off to Perugia on a £400,000 loan. The team remained unbeaten for a whole season, but drew so many times that they finished third. Then came the clandestine betting scandal; the three-year ban which was later cut to two; the three million dollar transfer back to Juventus; his reappearance on May 2nd 1982 just in time to claim a small share in Juventus League title; and glory in Spain. The 25-year-old who gleefully lifted the World Cup in Madrid had had more ups and down than a playground see-saw.

By comparison, Rummenigge's career seems almost boring. A steady progression since his Bundesliga debut in 1974 and his international

RUMMENIGGE

debut for West Germany against Wales in October 1976 saw "Kalle" piling up trophy after trophy. Individually, he's topped the scoring lists in the Bundesliga, and is now Bayern's second-highest scorer of all time behind the legendary Gerd Muller. He's averaged a goal for every two games throughout his career. His record includes title wins in the Bundesliga, the West German Cup, the European Cup, the Intercontinental Cup and the European Championship. In terms of honours, he beats Rossi hands down – but Paolo's modest collection of medals includes the big one that's missing from the Rummenigge trophy room – the World Cup winner's medal.

If Rummenigge's loyalty to Bayern contrasts sharply with Rossi's wanderings, it's also raised a few eyebrows among foreign clubs who've been prepared to pay big money for Kalle's services. "But I'm happy in Munich, and financially I have no reason to leave."

Certainly the five-year contract he signed in 1980 gave Rummenigge a just reward for his loyalty and an edge over Rossi in the money stakes. He's guaranteed £350,000 a year, and the numerous publicity deals involving his face or his signature bring in double that figure. Rossi on the other hand lost publicity deals hand over fist during his two-year ban, only to regain them just as quickly after his World Cup triumph and re-negotiate a new £250,000-a-year deal with Juventus. Goals, in any language, mean big money.

As personalities, Rossi and Rummenigge are different again. Tall, blond Rummenigge is quiet, modest and very much a low-key superstar. Success hasn't gone to his head, and his calm, balanced attitude to the game has kept him away from headline-grabbing controversies. Rossi is cheerful, modest and more extrovert than Rummenigge, but there's a cool, calculating brain ticking away behind those wide boyish eyes. Rossi has never been far away from controversy. Neither of them is a dominant

personality. On the field, you'll rarely see them organising a game or grabbing it by the scruff of the neck. They don't roast their team-mates or try to lift morale when things are going wrong. They'll change the course of a game with their goals.

Their playing styles also differ. Rummenigge's best form at Bayern has prospered in the team's 4-4-2 system, with Karl-Heinz running the left flank and looking for the fast counter-attack. Rossi is more at home in a 4-3-3 format that includes another tougher central striker in the mould of Graziani or Bettega.

For both of them, speed is the key. "I can't stand slow build-ups," says Rossi. "I like to play simple, fast football and to strike directly for goal." Rummenigge shares his opinion. Legendary Dutch left-winger Robby Rensenbrink says "I've seen more skilful Number 11s, but Rummenigge must be one of the most effective and efficient in the history of the game. He's fast over short and medium distances, and even when he's running with the ball, he's practically impossible to overhaul. What's more, people talk about all the goals that Rummenigge scores, but he's not a selfish player by any means, and sets up dozens of goals per season for midfielders who break through from deeper positions while the defence is concentrating on stopping him."

The average striker will score between two and three goals from every ten chances that come his way. Rossi and Rummenigge will convert between six and seven.

Rummenigge's striking rate owes a great deal to his studies of the great Gerd Muller at Bayern. Kalle has the same understanding of the art of goalkeeping, and somehow always produces a shot exactly where the keeper least wants it. He doesn't try to burst the ball with each shot, but his control and placing are exceptional. His repertoire ranges from cunning prods or deflections to spectacular overhead volleys, but the destination is always the same – the back of the net.

(Left) Rossi scores Italy's first goal in the 1982 World Cup Final. (Below) Rummenigge opens the scoring for West Germany in their friendly at Wembley.

Proud Kenny

Arsenal and England full-back
Kenny Sansom displays one of
his most treasured possessions –
the shirt of Karl-Heinz Rummenigge, the famous West German
striker. Kenny was presented
with the shirt following England's friendly with West Germany in 1982, which ended 2–1 in
the visitors' favour. Both goals
were scored by King Karl. Magnificent efforts which left Kenny
shaking his head in admiration.

'MOVE OVER, BOBBY MOORE'
—that's BRYAN ROBSON'S dream

I was a little lad of nine when England celebrated the greatest moment in their history – winning the World Cup.

The combined might of West Germany, Brazil and Argentina were powerless to stop Sir Alf Ramsey's team from storming to victory in the 1966 tournament.

England 4, West Germany 2 after a cliff-hanging climax to the game in extra-time. Who will ever forget that?

That magnificent achievement made the whole country go soccer daft. And I was no exception as Geoff Hurst, Bobby Moore, Bobby Charlton, Alan Ball and Nobby Stiles filled my scrapbook of heroes.

Amazingly, that all happened almost 20 years ago. That picture of Bobby Moore, the captain, clutching the World Cup, perched upon the shoulders of his victorious team-mates, went round the world.

It has been pulled from the files of photo-libraries at every opportunity, and it wouldn't surprise me if it is turning brown with age and over-use.

I was one of thousands of English soccer fans to cut that picture from the magazines and store it lovingly for posterity in my scrapbook.

Well, almost 20 year on, I have a serious confession to make. It's simply this . . .

I AM SICK TO DEATH OF SEEING THAT PICTURE.

It's about time England won the World Cup again to enable Bobby Moore and the rest to take a well-earned rest from the limelight.

We shall never, never forget what they did for England. They gave us the proudest moment in a long history of success, but it breaks my heart to think that England have only played in two World Cup Finals since winning the Cup in 1966.

I can remember dreaming of emulating the feats of England's World Cup winning team when I was a soccer-mad schoolboy.

Incredibly, all these years on, I find myself in with a chance of achieving what I believed to be the "impossible" – getting my hands on that Cup.

Isn't it time we gave the England fans a chance to pin another picture in their scrapbooks, alongside the famous one of Bobby Moore and his heroes?

My target for 1986 is two-fold. I want to captain England into action in the World Cup Finals, and, more ambitiously, lead England to glory in the World Cup Final.

But first we must qualify for the greatest show on earth — and my initial job is to retain my England form so that I'm in with a chance of achieving my objective.

It would be foolish to forecast glory for England when we failed to qualify for the 1974 and 1978 Finals, and struggled to get to Spain in 1982.

But I'm cautiously optimistic that England can build on the early promise we showed in the early months of Bobby Robson's managerial reign.

His decision to blood several exciting new players at international level with exciting results gives us good cause to look to the future with renewed optimism.

The so-called "Black Explosion" has thrust Cyrille Regis, Mark Chamberlain, Luther Blissett and Ricky Hill into the limelight, and the thrilling potential of Gary Mabbutt, Sammy Lee, Tommy Caton, Paul Goddard and Alan Devonshire should ensure success.

If we should qualify for the 1986 World Cup, many other candidates for an England place will have emerged. So the future looks brighter than it has ever been since Alf Ramsey's England were triumphant all those years ago.

Too many for my liking . . .

Whatever happens, we certainly won't be lacking in commitment. The England dressing-room is always bubbling before important games.

Standing in the centre will be big Terry Butcher and his Ipswich colleague Paul Mariner giving advice and geeing everyone up.

If the critics accused them of lacking commitment, they'd be likely to get a bloody nose.

Then there's Peter Shilton. He'll be well away from the two Ipswich lads telling the defenders exactly what to do at corners and free-kicks.

The future looks rosy for England just now, and by the time we start our 1986 World Cup matches we should have a good blend of youth and experience and we might just lift that trophy 20 years after Bobby Moore got his hands on it.

Tommy Caton shows there's more to him than defending when he scores the first of his two goals that gave Manchester City a 2-1 win over Arsenal in December 1982.

NOT JUST

Most people are wrong when they attempt to guess Tommy Caton's age. The problem stems from the fact that he is never as old as they expect him to be. But that's why Manchester City's dominant young centre-half believes he can become the best in the land.

Caton is only 22. It seems he has been around for a long time, but perhaps a League debut at 16 thanks to Malcolm Allison's ability to recognise natural talent has something to do with that.

"I was disappointed not to make the England squad for the 1982 World Cup.

Bryan jumps for joy after scoring the winner against Stoke City at Old Trafford

A GOAL-STOPPER

Big-headed? Not me. There are not too many genuine centre-halves on the scene these days, not like the days of Brian Labone, Jack Charlton, Larry Lloyd and Mike England.

"I'll always be grateful to Malcolm for throwing me in at the deep end. I was learning my profession when so many lads are still cleaning boots and waiting for their chance. I made mistakes, I learned from them and I played against some of Europe's most dangerous strikers.

"John Bond's arrival at Maine Road meant that everyone had to be on their toes. Competition for back-four places hotted up and I was determined to show him that I was first choice No. 5.

"The boss is hard but fair. He recognises effort and ambition and helped me tremendously."

Bobby Robson inherited a minor problem at the heart of England's defence when he succeeded Ron Greenwood as national manager. Terry Butcher, Russell Osman, Alvin Martin and Steve Foster were all given their chance. And by facing the fact that adjustments had to be made, Robson coped well. But Caton has been hammering on the door for more than a year.

"In the modern game the centre-half has to be more than just an old-fashioned stopper who battles with his opposing striker and misses out on a lot of build-up play. I like involvement, I want the ball and I like to break forward when the chance arises. I also recognise that I must return a certain percentage of goals per season and as long as I can maintain the standards set by City I am confident that I am good enough to become England's number one.

"I must keep believing this, otherwise I'll slip behind in the race." And I want to be leading it.

'HEAVY' HAMMER

Most players fight against putting on weight, but Alan Devonshire is an exception. He's worked hard at making himself heavier to carry on with starring for West Ham and to further his international ambitions with England. Now around 11 stone 6 lbs, Alan reckons it's the heaviest he's been, and enables him to shake off tackles more easily without robbing him of any of his electric pace.

It also provides more power to his shooting boots. He's very conscious of the fact that he still isn't hitting the back of the net as frequently as a player of his position is expected to do.

Alan has had a storybook rise to being ranked as one of the most stylish, and hardest to stop, attacking midfielders in the country. He was 26 before he was signed by The Hammers, after disappointments following trials with Crystal Palace and Q.P.R., and made his League debut shortly afterwards against West Bromwich Albion.

Formerly a fork-lift truck driver, playing part-time for Isthmian League club Southall, Alan has certainly risen in the world!

Everton's Graeme Sharp in a dynamic action pose.

Northern Ireland 'keeper Pat Jennings saves a blistering shot from Cyrille.

'How I can become ENGLAND'S FIRST CHOICE CENTRE-FORWARD'

BY CYRILLE REGIS

It is some measure of the progress Cyrille Regis has made at football's highest level when he now lays claim to a regular place in the England team.

West Bromwich Albion's powerful black centre-forward was a latecomer to the professional game. Signed for £5000 from amateur club Hayes in 1976, he was 20 when he made his League debut, scoring in a 3-0 win at Newcastle in September 1977.

But as Regis admitted: "I never served the usual apprenticeship as a pro and accept that many lads had already acquired two or three years League experience when I was a complete newcomer.

"I had to find my feet, especially playing in the First Division. But I listened to my team-mates, the manager and coach and watched other players in action. It took me time, but I think I eventually caught up."

That's an understatement. Having dismissed the chance of electing to play for France – Regis was born in French Guyana – he set his heart on winning some international recognition for England.

"I really wanted to be able to say that I'd made that grade. And when I won my first cap under Ron Greenwood, against Northern Ireland as a sub, I was proud enough to feel ten feet tall."

By then, however, Regis's ambitions had grown. His consistency in front of goal brought greater self confidence. And two further caps followed before injury cruelly robbed Regis of a chance of joining England's World Cup squad in Spain.

"When Greenwood retired and Bobby Robson took over, I worried a bit about perhaps having to prove myself all over again. But then Robson had made me captain of the Under-21 side once and he showed he'd hadn't discounted me by giving me cap number four against West Germany at Wembley."

PROGRESS

England lost 2-1 in that friendly. But Regis accepted that he had more work to do before Robson would select him in front of Paul Mariner.

"I've come a long way since leaving Hayes," said Regis, "and I have to keep reminding myself that I've made good progress on the international front. But I also have to achieve even greater consistency if I'm ever to be able to say that, injury apart, I'm England's number one centre-forward."

Hard work, yes, but with a track record like that of Cyrille Regis, it's odds-on that he will achieve his aim.

No mourning at Molineux

NOW IT'S WONDERFUL WOLVES

its place came young pride and ambition. Experienced pros like Kenny Hibbitt, Andy Gray and Geoff Palmer were persuaded to stay. The mixture was lethal to the rest of the Second Division.

"I admit I'd had enough and wanted to leave," said Gray: "but I was glad I saw things through because it was an exciting, rewarding season. The fans came back and we developed an incredible amount of young talent in one season."

Hibbitt added: "Those kids did us proud. I was delighted to give them all the benefits of my experience because I'd already developed a feeling for the club. I was a bit worried at first, but the way Derek Dougan set about things, leaving team matters to Graham Hawkins, left us in no doubt that here was a tidy ship once more."

ATTACKING FOOTBALL

Wolves' plight interested the rest of the clubs for more reasons than just sympathy. Too many League outfits were in financial trouble and it came as a great boost for the whole structure to see Wolves work their way out of trouble without spending money they did not have and by playing attacking football that produced goals and excitement, home and away.

It remains to be seen where Dougan and Hawkins can take their young Wolves, but they are boosted by the knowledge that they already represent one of football's modern survival miracles.

Clubs throughout Britain held their breath during the Summer of 1982 as the Official Receiver began the last day count-down on the fate of one of England's oldest clubs, Wolverhampton Wanderers.

The Wolves went bankrupt. And it was on the last day of the deadline before, as the Receiver threatened: "The bulldozers will move in on Molineux", that former playing idol Derek Dougan led a dramatic rescue team into the boardroom.

Wolves were saved, but only just. It seemed, however, that it would take an age of Second Division mediocrity, at best, to rebuild the once great club. But Dougan's impact was astonishing. He threw open the doors to the fans, appointed local-born former player Graham Hawkins as manager, took over the financial dealings himself and began ruling Molineux with the determined statement: "The buck stops with me. If I get it wrong we all go under. So I'm working day and night to see that I get it right."

He did. Wolves returned to basics with local youngsters replacing former stars, the wages bill was slashed and in

(Top) The man who has masterminded the Wolves revival – Derek Dougan.

(Left) Andy Gray decided to remain at Molineux – and hasn't regretted it!

PUZZLE CORNER

PUTTING THE 'CLU' IN CLUBS

Study these rhyming clues and name ten clubs, five English and five Scots. As a guide, the first has been answered for you.

1	If perchance you should be poor, These could lurk outside your door	**WOLVES**
2	Legendary yarns tell when This was home for Robin's men	
3	The place where guns and shot were made To come to war-torn country's aid	
4	If folks ignored you it just meant That to this place you had been sent	
5	Our mariners oft give this name To their sea-going vessel's frame	
6	It sounds as if we have right here A place that's full of atmosphere	
7	For news of home no need to pine, It sounds as if Mum's doing fine	
8	From Asia, it appears to say, Comes instrument that one can play	
9	Blessed things for which true lovers pine, Their patron saint is Valentine	
10	No Jack will do, and nor yet Johnny, The filmland partner's name was Bonnie.	

HAVING A BALL

By trial and error, find the correct starting points in each ring and, moving onto an adjacent space in a clockwise direction, spell out the names of 20 famous soccer clubs, 10 English and 10 Scottish.

SHATTERED DREAMS

Despair along the F.A. Cup trail.

There are no clues to this crossword frame. All the words you need to complete it are contained somewhere in the following:—

"THERE WAS NO ROAR AS BARNSLEY K.O.'D THE IDOLS OF ENFIELD AT WHITE HART LANE. IT IS NO LIE TO SAY THAT EVEN THE REF LOOKED SAD. BUT MANY A CUP HOPE ENDS IN THIS WAY."

SPOT THE DIFFERENCE

The artist has made ten alterations to both the reproductions on the right. Can you find them?

'FLASH IN THE PAN? NOT ME !'

declares
LUTHER
BLISSETT
(Watford)

All Watford's achievements since Graham Taylor took over will amount to nothing if the amazing Hertfordshire club fails to sustain its new-found position.

That's the forthright opinion of their England striker Luther Blissett, who also used the same logic to describe his own international future.

Blissett, of the explosive run and powerful, unpredictable shot, rattled a hat-trick as England destroyed little Luxembourg 9-0 at Wembley last year. But while describing it as "The most memorable moment of my career," Blissett was quick to add: "But I've got to at least sustain that standard if I'm to avoid being talked about in future years as someone who failed to live up to his early promise.

"Flash in the pan? Not me!

"Promotion all the way from Division Four to Division One was a phenomenal return for all the hard work the manager and players put in. The whole area came alive during that period as we dumbfounded our critics week after week.

"But having enjoyed a marvellous first season in the First Division, all that is now history. And we must match those achievements . . . then better them. The game is littered with one-off triumphs. We all want to establish a level of top-class consistency. That is when you are recognised as a team of real class."

HARD TRAINING

Not that Blissett underestimates his manager. Not for one second: "You must be joking! The boss is always ahead of the rest in our opinion. He worked a miracle at Vicarage Road and while the players – and the fans – played their part, it was Taylor who made it all happen.

"He will not allow us to falter. The training is hard at our place and the standards set are very high. Take my word for it, we are at an important crossroads and I look forward to helping Watford collect further honours.

"That's the only way to really get to the top. Liverpool set the pace for everyone, and the example. And you simply cannot do better than follow that example."

HIBS' HERO

When Jackie McNamara signed for Hibs he was slightly baffled . . . because the first he heard of the move was on his car radio!

"It may sound amazing, but it's true," insists Jackie, the Easter Road club's dynamic captain.

"I was with Celtic at the time and they were due to play Dundee United in a League Cup-tie at Parkhead. I had been the centre of transfer speculation for a few months when the then-manager Jock Stein told me to turn up before the game.

"As I arrived at Parkhead a sports programme came on the car radio and I was reliably informed a certain Jackie McNamara had signed for Hibs in a swop deal with Pat Stanton!

"Amazed? You can say that again! But I was happy enough with the news. I met Hibs' former manager Eddie Turnbull and the following day I went through to Edinburgh for my medical and to finalise details.

"I put pen to paper, but I'll tell you another little secret . . . I failed my medical!"

"I had been having trouble with a knee injury which refused to clear up. And, sure enough, the injury showed up again when I had an X-ray.

"However, Eddie Turnbull was so determined to sign me that he pushed the deal through . . . and I'm delighted he did.

"At first, though, I wondered if I had made the right decision. I was replacing Pat Stanton in the Hibs line-up and he was a legend with the Edinburgh fans.

"They weren't slow to tell me, either. Any time I made a mistake they immediately compared me with Pat and said things like 'he wouldn't make an error like that' and so on.

'DIDN'T WORK'

"But my old knee injury actually came to my rescue after about 18 games or so.

"It flared up again and manager Turnbull was forced to leave me out of the first team. The rest did me the world of good and when I came back the Hibs fans, thankfully, weren't still comparing me with Pat Stanton.

"I was able to get back into the side, settle into the scheme of things and take it from there. I've enjoyed myself at Easter Road and I hope there are more good days ahead.

"Pat Stanton, of course, is now my manager. Yes, it's a funny old game football, isn't it?"

Does McNamara have any regrets about not making the grade with Celtic? "I've got to say I feel a trace of bitterness about not becoming a regular at Parkhead," he says.

"I don't think I did myself justice with Celtic. Goodness knows I tried hard enough, but things just didn't work out.

"When it became obvious I wasn't going to get consistent first team football with Celtic I had to think about moving on.

"People talk about the glamour being involved with a big club like Celtic, but when I was out of the first team I was earning only something like £40 per week. Okay, that was some time ago, but I still had a family to feed.

"It was a wrench leaving Parkhead, but, looking back, I'm sure it was the right decision. Anyway, I didn't seem to have much say in the matter. I was 'transferred' even without my knowledge!"

Jackie McNamara (left) the Hibs' captain who figured in a surprising transfer from Celtic.

When we think of winning sequences many fans tend to recall Nottingham Forest's record-breaking run of 42 First Division games without defeat between losing 0-1 at Leeds on November 19th 1977, and 0-2 at Liverpool on December 9th 1978.

Forest's League record broke that created by Don Revie's Leeds United combination when they played 34 First Division games without defeat after losing 1-5 at Burnley on October 19th 1968, and before going down 2-3 at Everton on August 30th, 1969.

However, when it comes to *winning* sequences, surprisingly enough neither of these great sides come anywhere near the top in this regard.

The best First Division run since the War is that of Spurs who won 13 successive League games in 1960. This was the side that first proved the experts wrong by winning the League and Cup "double" under modern conditions. It was a feat that had not been performed for more than 60 years.

In Tottenham's winning sequence, they won the last two games of season 1959-60 before setting up a First Division record by winning the first 11 games of 1960-61. When they sunk Wolves 4-0 at Molineux to record their 13th win in a row (11th of the season) they were still no more than three points ahead of Sheffield Wednesday,

Spurs' double-winning side of 1961.

WINNING RUNS

the only other unbeaten First Division side at this stage.

Morton achieved 25 wins in succession in the Second Division of the Scottish League. Revitalised by the initiative of director-manager Hal Stewart, Morton began their run by winning the last two games of season 1962-63 and went on to win the first 23 games of 1963-64 before losing 1-3 to East Fife at Bayview Park. Their goals tally for these 25 games was 103 to 26!

Celtic fans may be thinking that their favourites might well have done better than this when they created another all-time record by playing 62 Scottish League games without defeat in seasons 1915-16 and 1916-17. Here again we can be misled, for although a fine run in itself the best Celtic could do for wins was 12 in a row!

Rangers had a run of 22 victories during seasons 1898-99 and 1899-1900.

The record run of victories in the Football League is one of 14. This was first created as long ago as 1904-05 by Manchester United and is a record which stands today, although it was equalled by Bristol City the following season and by Preston North End in 1950-51. All three clubs were in the Second Division.

Manchester United's victories were in a run of 18 games without defeat, while Bristol City at that time played 21 without defeat. The more recent Preston run was among 20 games played in succession without defeat.

When Bristol City won promotion to the First Division in 1976 one of the best-known TV commentators said something about it being their first spell among the soccer elite. Their earlier run of five seasons in Division One had long been forgotten, in the same way as the club's winning run which first won them promotion from the Second Division in 1905-06. The Manchester United side just mentioned hammered City 5-1 in the opening game at Clayton (United's old ground) and were to finish runners-up to the West Country club. Thereafter, City won 14 games and did not lose until beaten 1-2 at home by Leicester Fosse – City's only home defeat of this campaign.

GOAL-POACHER

No doubt many readers will consider Preston's record best of these three because it was achieved in a longer and more competitive season. Preston made an indifferent start to that season and even the transfer of centre-forward, Charlie Wayman, from Southampton did not have an immediate impact, but once this fast-moving and elusive goal-poacher had settled into the forward line of Tom Finney, Ken Horton, Bobby Beattie or Eddie Quigley and Angus Morrison,

there was no stopping Preston. A run of 20 games without defeat included those 14 successive victories, beginning with a 5-1 thrashing of Swansea.

Since 1970 there have been only three examples of a Football or Scottish League side winning more than 10 games in a row.

The best of these was Rangers in 1972-73 when they clocked up 16 First Division victories in succession. Yet this was not one of their numerous Championship-winning seasons, but one in which they finished a point behind Celtic at the top of the table. Rangers goals tally for those 16 games was 43-12 with Derek Parlane top scorer on 13.

Another Scottish side to finish Championship runners-up – Aberdeen in 1970-71, won 15 League games in a row and kept a clean sheet in a run of 12 of those games.

The most recent winning sequence worthy of mention was, not unexpectedly, performed by Liverpool. In 1981-82 when The Reds won the League for the fifth time in seven seasons, they chalked up a run of 11 victories. After their shock 0-1 defeat by Brighton at Anfield on March 6th, Liverpool did not drop another point until drawing 2-2 with Spurs at White Hart Lane on May 3rd. Here again the goals tally is worth noting 27-5. The goals in this spell were spread among no less than nine players with Craig Johnston top on six.

'Nightmare strikers fear'

Up front with STEVE ARCHIBALD

It's the nightmare all goalscorers fear. The time when the goals dry up . . .the time players like me dread.

Goalscorers are a special breed. They can destroy the best of defences with one flash of inspiration. They can win games and grab the glory.

Fans make enormous demands on soccer's most wanted men. But there isn't a striker in the world who hasn't experienced the nightmare of a barren goals spell.

Even the great Kenny Dalglish once went 25 League games spread over 11 months before scoring a goal. Yet he still made a valuable contribution to the Liverpool team.

I'm a notorious slow-starter. When I was at Aberdeen I played nine games at the beginning of season before opening my account.

Later, as a Spurs player, I ended the 1980/81 season as the First Division's top goalscorer with 25 goals, and followed up by hitting a bad patch halfway through the next season.

The last one wasn't particularly happy for me in the goalscoring stakes, either. At the halfway stage I had managed just four League goals, disastrous for a striker aiming to help Tottenham to top honours and secure a permanent place in the Scotland team.

In fact, it was Scotland manager Jock 'Stein who provided a real morale-booster just when I needed it most.

I was off form and worried about playing for Scotland in their European Championship clash against East Germany in October 1982, especially as I was carrying a groin strain.

I phoned Mr. Stein and told him I was injured and felt apprehensive.

"Nonsense," he boomed. "Pack your bags and join the squad and we'll see how bad it is. I want you in my team."

Those last six words made me feel on top of the world and restored a great deal of lost confidence.

When the goal-touch goes it can be really depressing. You can't find your rhythm. The harder you try the more difficult goal-scoring becomes. Shots that normally go in miss by inches, or bounce off defenders' legs.

It's essential to remember good players don't become bad ones overnight.

These lean spells are real tests of character for players. Some never recover and drift out of the game altogether.

It's important to keep looking for the ball, getting into good positions.

It's easy setting up chances when you are in the middle of a good run, but players who refuse to hide when the going gets rough are worth their weight in gold . . . or goals.

Garry Birtles is a good example. Following his £1,250,000 transfer from Nottingham Forest to Old Trafford in October 1980, Garry went 11 months and 30 League games before scoring his first goal for Manchester United.

Garry never really settled at United, but recovered his striking form soon after returning to Nottingham Forest in September 1982.

Tolerance and understanding from the fans is also important. The United supporters were fair to Garry because they could see he was doing his best.

Fortunately, the Spurs supporters have been magnificent to me. Whenever I've lost my touch, they've kept faith. They appreciate I'm giving 100 per cent and realise jeers will only increase the pressure and add to the problem.

The two other people I'm always grateful to are my team-mate Garth Crooks and my wife Maureen.

My striking partnership with Garth works well on and off the pitch. He never stops encouraging me and his chirpy good humour has often lifted the gloom.

I'm not the easiest of guys to live with and get bad-tempered at times. But Maureen understands the situation and helps me relax by taking me out for a meal.

Garth and Maureen are towers of strength when the nightmare strikes.

Steve holds off a Sunderland player to provide a team-mate with a goalscoring chance.

Aberdeen's international goalkeeper Bobby Clark blinked in utter astonishment back in season '76-'77 when his team's substitute Davie Robb suddenly emerged in front of a packed goalmouth to send a powerful close-range shot under goalkeeper Peter Latchford's body to leave Celtic hurtling to a 2-1 defeat in the League Cup Final at grey, old Hampden Park.

"It was an astonishing experience," says Clark. "I had actually 'seen' it all in my dreams the night before.

"I know it sounds unbelievable, but I told Davie Robb as we travelled to the game that he would come on as substitute and score the winning goal and we would emerge as 2-1 victors.

"That's precisely what happened. I don't know what Davie thought when I told him this, but he'll back up my story.

"My dream was so life-like I had to tell him. And when he came on as a late substitute and got that extra-time goal I had to rub my eyes to make absolutely certain I wasn't seeing things."

Arthur Graham, the Leeds United touchline flier, also remembers an Aberdeen Cup Final triumph over Celtic back in season '69-'70 when he was with the Pittodrie men.

"For a start, I didn't think I would be playing," confesses Graham. "I had only played a handful of first team games that season and I was surprised – shocked would probably be a better word – when the then-manager Eddie Turnbull told me I was in against the Celts in the Scottish Cup Final.

"We won 3-1 and you would have thought it would have been a real family occasion. But most of my brothers were upset . . . they're Celtic fans, you see!"

Tom Forsyth was another Cup Final hero against Celtic in a Scottish Cup Final ten years ago when Rangers beat the Parkhead side 3-2 in an electrifying match that had the ancient football fortress of Hampden rocking to its foundations.

"I'll never forget that afternoon," says Forsyth, currently managing Dunfermline. "I got the winning goal, of course, but I'll tell you a secret . . . I probably shouldn't have been playing."

Forsyth was carrying an injury at the time and such a knock would have ruled most players out of action, but he was determined to play against Celtic –

SHOOT Annual takes you behind the scorelines of Hampden Park Finals, to reveal tales that went unreported, stories that didn't hit the headlines. We bring you . . .

SECRETS OF THE STARS

Dundee United's Paul Hegarty holds up the Scottish League Cup for the second year in succession after beating Dundee at Dens Park. It was a repeat scoreline for United, having beaten Aberdeen by the same amount the previous year.

and got a handsome reward when he popped up near the end of the game to force the ball over the line after Derek Johnstone had hit the upright with a flying header.

Derek Johnstone certainly knows all about the cheers and the tears of Hampden showdowns, but he must surely be the only player to score a goal in such a game BEFORE IT WAS SCHEDULED TO KICK-OFF!

His memorable moment that shouldn't have been came against Hearts in season '75-'76.

He recalls: "We got a free-kick out on the right straight from the kick-off and Tommy McLean took it quickly, flighting it into the Hearts penalty box.

"I got up above their defence and nodded it down into the corner past goalkeeper Jim Cruickshank. It was only later that I was told I had scored that goal two minutes before three o'clock.

"The referee had kicked off early, but I wasn't complaining. And I wasn't grumbling at the end, either . . . I scored another and we won 3-1."

"I could hardly believe my ears. To say I wasn't too happy would be putting it very mildly indeed. As it turned out, Celtic won 3-2."

Fergie, however, had much better fortune when Aberdeen beat Rangers 4-1 in the Scottish Cup Final two season ago. Even when they lost the opening goal to a diving header from John MacDonald, Fergie revealed: "I wasn't dismayed.

"In fact, I had based most of my plans around Rangers scoring the first goal!

"I had told my players before the game not to go to pieces if the Ibrox side did take the lead. My lads took it all in their stride and, as everyone knows now, everything went our way at the end of the day."

Cup Finals also tend to throw up odd facts . . . like the day in season '74-'75 when Joe Harper hit a superb hat-trick for Hibs against Celtic in the League Cup Final . . . and still finished up on the losing side!

Dixie Deans got a hat-trick for Celtic that day . . . and realised lightning could strike twice in the same place.

Three years earlier Deans played for Celtic against the Easter Road side in the Scottish Cup Final at Hampden – and drilled in another unstoppable hat-trick as the Parkhead giants swept to a landslide 6-1 triumph.

And what about the team that twice

Johnstone, however, was on the receiving end in season '70-'71 when, after scoring a last-minute equaliser to force a replay, he saw the Ibrox men lose 2-1 to old foes Celtic.

One man with a happy memory of that evening, though, was little Lou Macari, who was then breaking into the Parkhead first team.

Macari netted Celtic's first goal and was quite candid afterwards when asked about his effort.

"I was confident of scoring," said the impish Macari. "In fact, I would ALWAYS be confident of scoring against Rangers! It wasn't anything special, a close-range shot after a corner on the left, but it brought me one of my first medals in the game."

Another Celt with fond memories of a Cup triumph over Rangers is George Connelly.

Jock Stein catapulted him into the Celtic forward line back in '68-'69 as a raw youngster when he took the place of Jimmy Johnstone at outside-right.

Stein, the wily, old fox, had laid his trap perfectly and used Connelly in a midfield role. By the time Rangers had worked out the switch Celtic were cruising to a 3-0 half-time lead . . . and Connelly was one of their marksmen.

John Greig, under pressure, was robbed of the ball about 25 yards from goal by the gifted Fifer. The occasion and the pressure might have got to Connelly as he advanced down upon goalkeeper Norrie Martin, but, staying remarkably composed and calm, he walked the ball round the Ibrox number one and, with nonchalant ease, rolled in goal number three.

Stevie Chalmers added a solo fourth goal in an overwhelming 4-0 victory and Jock Stein's shared "secret" with Connelly was undoubtedly the major deciding factor on the day.

On that same afternoon Alex

(Above) Lou Macari celebrates one of his most magical moments – scoring the first goal in Celtic's 1971 Cup win over Rangers. (Right) Celtic's Dixie Deans collected another memorable hat-trick against Hibs in his club's 6-1 win in a 1972 Final.

Ferguson, who wasn't to know it at the time, of course, was playing his last game for Rangers! That was a secret he could have lived quite happily without . . .

Ferguson, the Aberdeen manager, was told to follow Celtic captain Billy McNeill everywhere when the Parkhead side gained a corner-kick.

"Celtic got a corner in the first minute and, would you believe, Billy scored with a header," groans Fergie. He was on the way out after that.

In fact, Alex Ferguson doesn't have many happy memories of Cup Final day when Celtic provide the opposition.

When Fergie was with Dunfermline they came up against Celtic in the Scottish Cup Final of '64-'65.

"I had been playing quite well at the time and scoring a few goals," recalls Fergie. "I thought I would be in the team, but I was absolutely flabbergasted when the East End Park manager at the time, Willie Cunningham, told me I was being left out.

won the League Cup on the ground of their fiercest rivals?

Dundee United fill that bill after winning the League Cup two years in succession at Dens Park, home of city opponents Dundee. They took it for the first time in '79-'80 after drawing 0-0 with Aberdeen at Hampden.

The replay was switched to Dens Park to enable more fans to travel to the midweek match and United promptly devastated The Dons with a thrilling 3-0 victory to clinch their first major trophy in 50 years.

A year later they were back at Dens Park in the Final of the same trophy . . . and again they won by the same scoreline although, this time, the team on the receiving end were Dundee.

Twelve months later United again battled through to the League Cup Final, but this time the game was held at Hampden with Rangers in contention.

The magic spell was broken – and United lost 2-1. Ironically, the winning goal came in the last minute from Ian Redford . . . a former DUNDEE player!

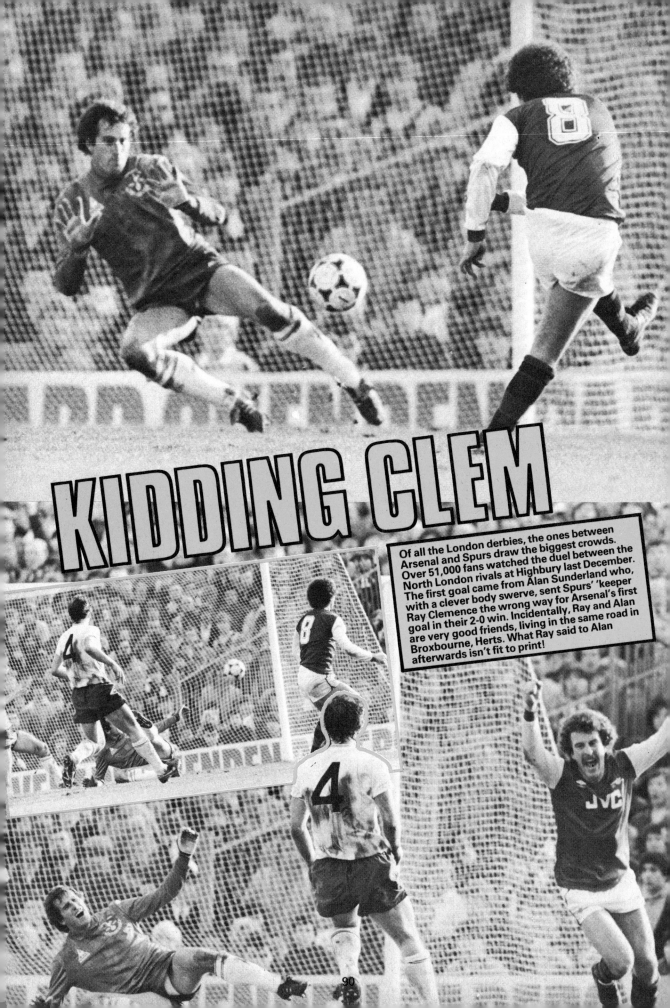

KIDDING CLEM

Of all the London derbies, the ones between Arsenal and Spurs draw the biggest crowds. Over 51,000 fans watched the duel between the North London rivals at Highbury last December. The first goal came from Alan Sunderland who, with a clever body swerve, sent Spurs' 'keeper Ray Clemence the wrong way for Arsenal's first goal in their 2-0 win. Incidentally, Ray and Alan are very good friends, living in the same road in Broxbourne, Herts. What Ray said to Alan afterwards isn't fit to print!

I've achieved a great deal of success with Aston Villa since making my first team debut as a 17-year-old substitute at Bristol City at the beginning of the 1978-79 season.

Championship, European Cup, Player of the Year awards and England recognition. Few players have made such an early impact in a career.

Yet despite all those highlights my future has been in jeopardy on several occasions because I failed to apply myself.

Soon after establishing myself in the Villa team I was taught a very valuable lesson . . . to work harder and strive for higher standards all the time.

I did tend to be a little lazy. These days no player, especially a striker, can afford to stand around waiting for things to happen.

There is no room in the modern game for posers who try to hide when the going gets rough.

You've got to work, work, work for the team if you want to achieve anything.

Fortunately Ron Saunders, who have me my big break at Villa, spotted the shortcomings in my game before it was too late.

He took me to one side after training one day and told me he was dissatisfied with my performances.

Mr. Saunders explained it was essential to keep on the move, showing myself for diagonal balls and be ready for the quick dash into the penalty-box.

"It's all a question of being aware," he said. "And maintaining concentration."

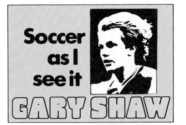

Soccer as I see it

GARY SHAW

I've never forgotten that advice and made sure that I got in and around the box more to improve my finishing power.

At the end of that 1980-81 season I ended as Villa's top scorer with 20 goals to help them win the Championship. I also played for the England Under-21's and was voted the P.F.A. Young Player of the Year. Proof enough that it pays to listen to advice.

My game was also given a boost when Peter Withe joined Villa from Newcastle in May, 1980.

I've learnt so much from big Peter just by watching him in training. His enthusiasm, determination and competitiveness are incredible.

Even in five-a-sides Peter will contest every ball, argue every decision that goes against him.

Peter doesn't hold back. He's given me many a verbal blasting for missing a goal. Football to Peter Withe is all about winning whether it's at Wembley or Bodymoor Heath, Villa's training ground on the outskirts of Birmingham.

On the field Peter always makes himself available. This takes pressure off the midfielders, making their job easier because he's always there to be hit. The ideal target man.

Peter also removes a tremendous amount of pressure. He takes the stick,

'ADVICE THAT SAVED MY CAREER'

Ron Saunders, the previous manager of Aston Villa who guided Gary.

leaving me free to "float" around, picking up his flicks and touches.

He has also taught me to retain confidence when the goals stop going in.

It's vital when the luck's out to get your head down, grit your teeth and get on with the game, still trying to make yourself available and creating chances.

I've had a fantastic start to my career, but success has brought problems of another kind.

People expect me to sustain my top form. Fall a little below par and I'm crucified.

I don't believe all the talk about being a superstar. I keep my feet on the ground. I've seen so many players destroy themselves trying to live up to reputations they don't deserve.

My advice to any reader aiming to make football a career is to work constantly at his game and don't cheat in training.

I still look at other players, trying to pick up tips. I never stop learning!

I still remember his role in helping the national side to reach the 1966 World Cup Final against England at Wembley.

Despite losing and being so young, Franz shone as a great star in the making.

He was also instrumental in knocking England out of the 1970 competition. Once the shackles were released when Bobby Charlton was substituted, Kaiser unleashed an unstoppable shot from the edge of the area to pull the Germans back to 1-2 and then helped them to eventually win 3-2 in the Quarter-Finals.

Those performances were from the midfield position and when he reverted to centre-back, all the class that he possessed shone through.

He was never afraid to go forward and was an ideal captain because he drove his team on by example and sheer class.

He was never afraid either to hit a long pass and was strong in the tackle . . . the sign of a great player.

Manchester United's Arnold Muhren.

"GEORGE MADE A STADIUM BUZZ"

GARY OWEN (WEST BROMWICH ALBION)

George Best (left is top of Gary Owen's football popularity poll.

I was fortunate enough to grow up as a Manchester United supporter during the heady days of Bobby Charlton, Denis Law and George Best.

It is the latter that I would travel all over the country to watch.

Whenever the likeable Irishman got the ball a buzz would spread all over the stadium.

George was the idol of everyone who stood on the Stretford End.

My only regret is that I never actually played against the Northern Ireland international.

I still remember his superb performance during the 1968 European Cup Final when Manchester United beat Benfica from Portugal at Wembley Stadium.

The game was finely balanced at 1-1 when the genial Irishman received the ball and went on to score a memorable goal to put the Old Trafford club 2-1 in front.

United eventually won 4-1 after extra-time to become the first English club to win the European Cup.

Yes, it is a pity there are not more superstars like George Best in the Football League today.

"BECKENBAUER – THE IDEAL CAPTAIN"

KEN MCNAUGHT (ASTON VILLA)

Although I have never played against Franz Beckenbauer (below) he is my favourite player.

The former West Germany star oozes class and confidence and this showed in his many games at club and international level.

Franz Beckenbauer.

"I LEARN FROM WATCHING ARNOLD MUHREN

KEVIN O'CALLAGHAN (IPSWICH TOWN)

Even though the club suffered a major blow when Arnold Muhren left Ipswich Town to join Manchester United in the summer of 1982 the likeable Dutchman is still top of my football pops.

92

PLAYER'

Five stars explain why they placed a particular player above all others in SHOOT magazine's popular Focus feature.

I learnt more about how the game is played by watching Arnold than any other player.

He is a winger's dream. When I played with him in the Ipswich side, he was always looking for me with those probing passes between the full-backs which is a trademark of Arnold's.

He is one of the best passers of a ball in the game.

I used to stay behind after training and invariably Arnold would still be there.

Some of the things he did with a ball were unbelievable.

He is still mised around Portman Road and Ipswich Town's loss is definitely Manchester United's gain.

His performances for the Old Trafford club bear out what I am saying about the international midfield star.

"EDDIE GRAY – BRILLIANT AND HONEST"

ALAN CURTIS (SWANSEA)

Even though I spent only 18 months with Leeds United, the one person who stood head and shoulders above anyone else was Eddie Gray (below).

I have played with and against Eddie and I must admit he is one class player.

I believe, from talking to the staff at Elland Road, that the player-manager is even more honest than when he was just a player.

During my spell there, the best game the Scottish international had was against Southampton at The Dell in a First Division game.

He was absolutely brilliant as United beat Lawrie McMenemy's Saints 2-1.

He is a player who could fill almost any position. He has played left-back, in midfield and on the wing.

Although I have not spoken to him much since he became player-manager at the start of the 1982-83 season, I am sure that if I ever became disillusioned with football and needed someone to talk to then Eddie would be only too willing to make himself available.

He is that sort of guy. A genuine, honest man.

"GLENN HODDLE – I WOULD TRAVEL TO SEE HIM"

NIGEL CALLAGHAN (WATFORD)

I have always been a great fan of Tottenham and England's stylish midfield player Glenn Hoddle.

I have marvelled at his tremendous skill for a long time, even though he is only in his mid-20's.

Eddie Gray of Leeds United.

Glenn Hoddle (right), a player of tremendous skill.

Glenn can hit a pass from anywhere on the park and it very rarely goes astray.

I remember his inch-perfect pass to Garth Crooks in the 1980-81 F.A. Cup Semi-Final replay against Wolves at Highbury.

From a defensive position Glenn split the Wolves defence with the perfect ball and Crooks was away and brilliantly tucked the ball in the net to help Spurs reach the Final.

And Hoddle also scores more than his share from a midfield position.

He has got some cracking goals in his time and is particularly dangerous with free-kicks around the penalty-area.

He has the skill to strike the ball with either foot and can bend the ball round most defensive walls.

I am a little surprised he has not won more England caps but he was sidelined a lot last season with niggling injuries.

Yes, Glenn Hoddle is still my favourite player and one I would travel a long way to see in action if I was not involved professionally.

Clive's father was also an accomplished goalscorer. Here he's shown scoring for Spurs in their 13-2 win over Crewe Alexandria in 1960.

Following in father's footsteps
CLIVE ALLEN

"The Son of Les" – that's the tag that dogged my early career.

When you are the son of a famous footballer you can't blame people for making comparisons.

It never worried me, even when fans came up to me after games and told me I wasn't a patch on my father, Les Allen.

In fact, Dad's reputation made me even more determined to succeed in my own right and equal if not better his achievements.

Dad's professional career started in 1954 and he played for Chelsea, Spurs, and Q.P.R., winning First, Second and Third Division Championship honours as well as F.A. Cup and League Cup winner's medals. So I've a great deal to live up to.

Because of Dad's involvement in the game I grew up in a total football environment. There was only one career to me . . . to follow in my father's bootsteps.

Having a famous player for a father has proved a great help because when I was growing up he was always talking about the game, giving me advice, warning of the pitfalls and dangers to avoid.

One of Dad's closest friends was former Tottenham manager Bill Nicholson. He and Dad often took me to White Hart Lane to watch games. I don't know if I should admit this, but I became a firm Spurs fan and still have more than a soft spot for the club.

Even our neighbours in Hornchurch where I grew up were well-known players. As a lad I lived in the same road as West Ham stars Geoff Hurst, Martin Peters and Ronnie Boyce, who is a coach at Upton Park.

Jimmy Greaves also lived in nearby Upminster and was a frequent visitor to the Allen home. So was Terry Venables, eventually to become my manager at Crystal Palace and Q.P.R.

During the school holidays Dad took me along to Q.P.R., where he was manager at the time, to watch training. The atmosphere of a big-time League club made me even more determined to become a professional.

But it wasn't all football for young Clive Allen. My father made me realise how important it was to concentrate on my school studies.

He used to say: "You won't always be a footballer. A good education is essential."

I took his advice and went on to gain 6 G.C.E. O levels apart from several C.S.E.'s.

Dad also ensured I stood on my own two feet and made my own decisions.

When I was at school, Arsenal, Spurs, Ipswich and Q.P.R. were all keen on me.

I finally chose Rangers because their manager at the time, Dave Sexton, much such an impression on me, and I could still live at home.

Having the family around was important to a 15-year-old about to step out into the wide world.

"Dave will look after you," Dad said. "You won't go wrong with him."

I was certainly glad to have Dad around a few years later when Arsenal signed me for £1 million and then sensationally sold me to Crystal Palace before I had played a single League game for them.

It was a traumatic experience and could well have seriously damaged my future career.

Dad's past experience as a player and manager helped me take everything in my stride.

He also shielded me from the Press to ensure I didn't say anything I might regret later. I dread to think what would have happened had I been with one of the big Northern clubs at that time and on my own.

The Arsenal episode is forgotten now, so is my unhappy spell at Crystal Palace when nothing seemed to go right.

I'm very happy back at the Rangers, where Dad, my wife Lisa and 11-year-old brother Bradley, another striker in the making, are regular visitors.

Dad's my biggest fan . . . and critic. He'll soon tell me what I've done wrong in a game.

I don't look for praise because he's always told me not to regard myself as someone special.

"Don't let any superstar nonsense affect your career," he once said.

In my case, following in father's footsteps has been a blessing.

HOPE YOU GET WELL STONED TONIGHT

ALL LIT-UP!

WHO'S BEEN A Tk-ooh! NAUGHTY BOY

EXIT

One way the game is keeping up with the times is by introducing electronic scoreboards to inform and excite the fans.

(Above) Watford fans are given the excuse to paint the town red following their 4-1 win over Brighton in the League last November.

(Left) Kenny Sansom of Arsenal got the message when he was sent to the sin-bin for a spell during a six-a-side tournament in Birmingham.

(Below) The sign that Danes appreciate good football — the word that greeted Trevor Francis' first goal in England's 2-2 draw last September. (Right) The Americans believe in applauding every good move!

WOW

DANMARK 0
1 ENGLAND

en-din kaffesmag

GIVE THAT MAN A HAND!

McSTAYING POWER!

PAT CRERAND with pace ... that's the description that so aptly fits Celtic's supremely-gifted teenage midfielder Paul McStay.

McStay, capped at almost every level by Scotland, is destined to become one of the game's greats, but the avalanche of praise that has been heaped upon his young shoulders has not affected him in any way.

As he emerged last season as a precocious 18-year-old and was immediately labelled a superstar by adoring fans there were no thoughts of flash cars or luxury houses:

Level-headed Paul, instead, preferred to stay with his parents in their small council house in Lanarkshire. And his Mum pointed out: "We don't spoil him in any way. He still shares the same bedroom with his other two brothers."

Paul, whose great uncle Willie was a Celtic star of the distant past, is certainly heading in the right direction and he says simply and logically: "I don't know what I would do without football.

"It always seemed that it would be my career and, thankfully, things have worked out okay so far.

"Celtic are a fabulous team. I've always supported them and it's just wonderful to play in that famous green-and-white jersey. And what can I say about the Parkhead fans?

"They are magnificent. They welcomed me into the first team right from the start and always encouraged me."

Celtic manager Billy McNeill pulled off yet another masterstroke when he introduced McStay to his midfield in place of veteran Dominic Sullivan.

In true storybook fashion McStay scored a magnificent goal in his Premier Division debut two seasons ago against Aberdeen at Pittodrie ... and he hasn't looked back since.

IN A HURRY

"I was very wary of pushing the boy too far," admits McNeill. "I didn't want him to burn himself out and I didn't want to put too much pressure on him.

"My fears were unfounded. He went into the team like he had played there all his life."

McNeill coaches the youngster along carefully, but McStay is the type of player who thrives on responsibility.

"I love hitting passes on target," he says with undisguised pride. "I'm willing to take a chance and go for a long pass and when it lands where I intended I'm delighted."

McStay simplifies his role in the Celtic formation, but he blends in so well with the equally-subtle and lavishly-skilled Tommy Burns and the hard-working Murdo MacLeod, who terrorises defences with his ferocious shooting.

Younger readers may not remember too much about Pat Crerand, who made his name with Celtic before transferring those talents to Manchester United in the Sixties where he won a European Cup medal in '68.

You can take it from us that Crerand could probably have threaded a pass through the eye of a needle ... and Paul McStay has that outstanding ability, too.

Plus, of course, he has pace. Yes, Paul McStay is certainly a youngster in a hurry!

Festive Fun

"It's my Christmas gift to the team – something they haven't seen much of lately."

"Here they come, Joe – the Three Wise Men."

"I hope the team's turkeys are tough – their pudding's brick-hard and their crackers all duds."

"What a lovely original present, dear – a notebook, pencil and a brand new whistle."

"Before I take this penalty – I'd like to wish you a Merry Christmas."

"Our first aid men decided to put on a special service during the Christmas games."

"Come here, Santa Claus."

The best performance by a British team in the European Championship was achieved by England when they finished in third place in the 1968 tournament. But hopes are justifiably high than in the 1984 Finals staged in France either England, the Republic of Ireland or one of the other home nations could win the trophy for the first time.

England created one record in the competition when in the qualifying match against Luxembourg on December 15th, 1982, at Wembley their 9-0 win was the biggest score in the history of the series.

Earlier on the same afternoon, Wales had gallantly drawn 4-4 in Yugoslavia in what was the highest scoring draw produced in the European Championship.

Northern Ireland's finest moment in Europe had come in their commendable single goal win over West Germany, who have been the most successful country in the competition, winning the title in 1972 and 1980.

Like the European Champion Clubs Cup, the European Nations Cup, as it was first called, made only a tentative start to its existence in 1958. Only 17 different nations entered.

Among the non-starters were the four home countries, and West Germany, Italy, Holland and Belgium, but there was full support from the Eastern European bloc.

On April 5th, 1959, the Republic of Ireland side beat the Czechs 2-0 but lost 4-0 in the return game staged in Bratislava on May 10th.

With home and away scores counting towards an aggregate for the winners, France were the leading marksmen in the First Round proper. They beat Greece 7-1 in their home leg and also drew 1-1 away.

In the Quarter-Finals there was a political row when the USSR were paired with Spain; although the cause

Can one of them win the European Championship for the first time ever?

of it, Spain's Civil War, had ended over twenty years before.

The Spaniards withdrew leaving the Soviet Union to walk over into the Semi-Finals where they met Czechoslovakia in Marseilles, since the Semi-Final stage was held in France. The Russians won 3-0 but the other game in Paris was a nine-goal thriller involving the hosts and Yugoslavia.

Yugoslavia prevailed 5-4 against the French and after the Czechs had beaten a disappointed French team 2-0 in the match for third place, the Soviet Union met Yugoslavia in the Final.

On July 10th, 1960, the Russians made a bad start with their captain and Master of Sport Igor Netto putting through his own goal to give the Yugoslavs the lead. But their equaliser forced extra-time in which Victor Ponedelnik scored the winning goal.

However, the Parisiens were not happy about their side failing to reach the Final which was watched by a disappointing crowd of 17,966. Despite

this there was little doubt that the competition had been a success and increased entries were expected for the second series which covered the period 1962-64.

Although 29 teams entered, the absentees included West Germany and Scotland. The other three home countries were represented, England and Wales failed at the First Round and only Northern Ireland succeeding in reaching Round Two.

Again a home and away knock-out system was used. Because of the uneven number of teams several byes had to be given and Greece's withdrawal gave Albania a walk-over into the Second Round.

The Irish impressed by beating Poland 2-0 at home and away and were only narrowly beaten by Spain 2-1 on aggregate. But England's First Round elimination came from an improved France and was a shock for new manager Alf Ramsey.

Wales had not been disgraced by

Luther Blissett scores one of the goals that gained him a hat-trick in England's record win over Luxembourg. It was Luther's first full game for his country's senior side.

losing to Hungary, but Scotland had been an odd absentee in what was becoming a more popular competition match by match.

The holders Russia, who had not played in the First Round, beat Italy in the Second and Sweden in the Quarter-Finals where the Spanish beat Eire and Denmark accounted for Luxembourg after a play-off to reach the last four with Hungary who had knocked out the French.

Spain was chosen as the venue for the Semi-Final period onwards and in Barcelona, Russia had a three clear goals win over Denmark. Spain had a tougher time against the Hungarians but prevailed by the odd goal in three.

After Hungary had beaten Denmark 3-1 after extra time in the match for third place, the Final in Madrid on June 21st, 1964, brought a confrontation between Spain the hosts and Russia the holders. This time there was no political intervention and the game provided Spain with considerable compensation as they emerged as 2-1 winners.

Any lingering suspicion that the European Nations Cup was not to become a huge success was dispelled by the crowd for the Final which numbered 120,000 and persuaded most of the other countries who had not joined in to enter for the next series – including the Scots!

UEFA decided to change the title of the competition and it became the European Football Championship for the 1966-68 tournament.

The initial stages were decided on a group League basis and the thirty-one entries were split into eight groups. With West Germany in their first Championship, they were fortunately drawn in the one group with three teams only.

But they were in for an unpleasant surprise. They could do no better than draw 0-0 in Albania and this loss of a precious point allowed Yugoslavia to qualify from this group.

With all four home countries listed among the contestants for the first time, the British International Championship was used over a two-year period as a qualifying group for the tournament.

England emerged as the winners despite being shaken in 1967 at Wembley when Scotland defeated them 3-2 to record the first defeat sustained by the World Cup winners, thus ending a run of 19 matches including the World Cup Final itself without defeat.

CHARLTON GOAL

A year later England's 1-1 draw at Hampden was sufficient to see them through as head of the group.

The other seven teams to reach the last eight were Spain, Yugoslavia, France, Italy, Bulgaria, the USSR and Hungary all strong contenders. England had a difficult task in the Quarter-Final draw against the holders Spain.

A goal by Bobby Charlton at Wembley gave England a narrow lead to take to the return game in Spain a month later in May. Ramsey gambled on a defensive based counter-attack game and it proved just right for the occasion. Norman Hunter in a No. 11 shirt even scored in England's 2-1 win, with Martin Peters registering the other goal.

The Quarter-Finals also saw the Yugoslavs repeat their 1960 success against the French while Russia narrowly defeated Hungary for their third Semi-Final place in succession and Italy completed the foursome by eliminating Bulgaria.

Italy was given the honour of staging the Semis but it was to be an unpleasant experience for England to be drawn against Yugoslavia in Florence. In a dramatic, tensely-fought encounter, Alan Mullery became the first full England international player to be sent off and in the last minute Dragan Dzajic scored Yugoslavia's winning goal.

By this time, of course, Italian football was well steeped in its blanket defensive system of catenaccio and they held the Russians to a goalless draw in Naples. However it was decided to toss a coin for the team to reach the Final and nobody was really surprised when the Italians won the right!

England beat the USSR 2-0 for third place with goals from Bobby Charlton and Geoff Hurst in a side containing eight of the World Cup winning team of two years earlier.

The Final on June 8th was another sterile battle between the Italians and Yugoslavia and it ended 1-1 in Rome. The match was replayed two days later, but this time goals by Luigi Riva and Pietro Anastasi saw the Italians bring the cup to their home country.

There was a similar formula of group matches for the 1972 series and with 32 entries representing the biggest number attracted to date, they were equally divided in eight groups.

On this occasion the draw split the four home countries, Wales competing with Rumania, Czechoslovakia and Finland; England with Switzerland,

(Below) A shock for England. They lost 3-1 to West Germany in 1972 at Wembley. (Right) Italy's captain holds the Cup on high following his country's Final win in 1968.

April, 1972
England 1, W. Germany 3
– HUMBLED AT WEMBLEY!

June, 1968
Italy 2, Yugoslavia 0
– WON ON THEIR HOME SOIL!

Greece and Malta; Northern Ireland against the USSR, Spain and Cyprus and Scotland against Belgium, Portugal and Denmark.

And while the Welsh, Irish and Scots could finish no higher than third in their respective groups, England won their section to reach the Quarter-Finals along with Rumania, Hungary, the USSR, Belgium, Italy, Yugoslavia and the West Germans, then building up what was to prove their most formidable squad.

And it was England's misfortune to clash with the Germans who were irresistible winners at Wembley in their 3-1 success, and though Ramsey's men earned an honourable draw in the return game, there was no disputing that the Germans had earned full revenge for their 1966 World Cup defeat.

Belgium surprised the Italians by the odd goal, Russia beat Yugoslavia in comfortable fashion, but the Hungarians needed a play-off to eliminate Rumania.

And it was Belgium which was chosen as the host country for the Semi-Finals which saw the USSR defeating Hungary by a single goal in Brussels and West Germany edging out the hosts 2-1 in Antwerp.

The Belgians did succeed in taking third place also by the odd goal in three at the expense of the Hungarians, but the scene was set on June 18th for a memorable Final between the increasing might of West Germany and the resilient Russians.

In the end it was a relatively comfortable success for the Germans who with two goals from Gerd Muller became impressive 3-0 winners of the European crown. With Gunter Netzer commanding midfield, Franz Beckenbauer organising the defensive and offensive operations and the diminutive Muller providing the clinical finishing, this combination proved too strong for the Soviet side.

By 1976 England were under the direction of a new manager in Don Revie. But after initial success against the Czechs, it was the Eastern bloc countries who qualified for the later stages not England. The home countries were well represented by Wales who qualified under the direction of Mike Smith topping a group above Hungary, Austria and Luxembourg and dropping just two points in the process.

Northern Ireland, who finished second in their section and Scotland who were third in theirs, again failed to reach the second stage of the competition.

The other Quarter-Finalists turned out to be familiar names in the history of the competition. Namely, Yugoslavia, Spain, Holland, the USSR, Belgium and West Germany the holders.

Germany beat Spain, the Czechs overcame their fierce Russian rivals and Holland gained the advantage over neighbours Belgium, while Yugoslavia defeated the gallant Welsh.

PENALTY DRAMA

The Semi-Finals held in Yugoslavia were packed with drama. Czechoslovakia needed extra-time to beat the Dutch 3-1 and West Germany recovered from being two goals down at half-time to force extra-time and an eventual 4-2 win over Yugoslavia with Muller scoring three goals.

Holland deprived the hosts of third place by beating them 3-2, but again it required extra time to settle the issue. In The Final on June 20th in Belgrade a last-minute equaliser by Bernd Holzenbein levelled matters for the Germans against Czechoslovakia, but the score remained at 2-2 even after the extra period.

Then came the drama of the penalty competition which Czechoslovakia won 5-3.

For the sixth Championship tournament there were several changes. Hitherto there had been no seeding or exemption for the host nation. This time there were seven group qualifiers to join Italy, the hosts.

England were placed in the same qualifying group as Northern Ireland and the Republic of Ireland plus Bulgaria and Denmark. They dropped only one point in their programme. But Scotland could only finish fourth in a group won by Belgium and Wales were third in a section headed by West Germany.

The other teams to reach the final stages were Greece, Czechoslovakia, Holland and Spain. This time it was the host country who held the remainder of the tournament.

Four venues were used for the matches: Rome, Naples, Turin and Milan with the match for third place being staged in Naples and the Final in Rome. England, Belgium, Spain and Italy were placed in one group; Czechoslovakia, West Germany, Greece and Holland in the other one.

The teams played each other once with the winners playing in the Final and the respective runners-up disputing third and fourth place.

For the third consecutive tournament there were 32 entries and although 33 different countries had played in the European Championship, they had not all managed to do so together.

Goals proved hard to come by in both Final groups. In fact the twelve games produced only 20 goals between them. Italy failed to score against Spain but the match ended scoreless and a late goal from Marco Tardelli ended England's hopes against them.

England did beat Spain 2-1 but it was Belgium who topped the group and won the right to meet West Germany, clear winners of the other group. Czechoslovakia were runners-up and beat Italy for third place.

The Final in Rome on June 22nd saw the Germans overturn Belgium 2-1.

For the seventh and present series, all 33 eligible members of UEFA have entered teams. France as the hosts are again excused for the qualifying period and the structure will be as for the sixth competition.

What a boost it would be for one of our five nations to become Kings of Europe!

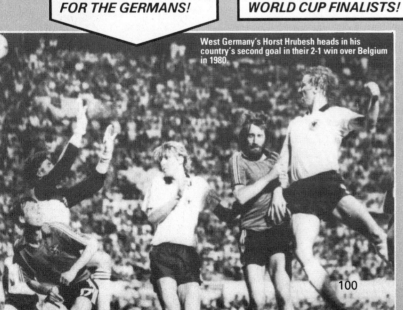

June, 1980
W. Germany 2, Belgium 1
— SECOND TROPHY WIN FOR THE GERMANS!

November, 1982
N. Ireland 1, W. Germany 0
— IRISH BEAT WORLD CUP FINALISTS!

In a qualifying match for the 1984 competition, Northern Ireland hit a high spot by beating West Germany 1-0 in Dublin. Scorer Ian Stewart duels with Uli Stielike.

West Germany's Horst Hrubesh heads in his country's second goal in their 2-1 win over Belgium in 1980.

Davie MacKinnon switched on his television to watch a sports programme and was left open-mouthed in astonishment . . .

The reporter announced to the nation that MacKinnon, then with Partick Thistle, had been forced to quit the game after undergoing an operation to remove a kidney.

"I was absolutely flabbergasted," admits MacKinnon. "I wondered what it was all about.

MacKINNON'S NO QUITTER!

"As far as I was concerned at the time I was looking forward to easing my way back into training and then trying to get back into the Thistle first team.

"Thoughts of chucking the game hadn't even entered my head. I had a chat with former Firhill manager Berti Auld and he, too, was more than just slightly surprised by the "news".

"Thankfully, it was all a misunderstanding."

The reporter in question must flush with embarrassment today when he sees MacKinnon in the thick of the action, playing with vigour and aggression . . . AND FOR RANGERS!

MacKinnon's rags-to-riches story was complete when the famous Ibrox side bought him from Thistle before the start of last season.

Manager John Greig was on the look-out for a replacement for the right-back berth that had been vacated by Sandy Jardine, given a free transfer after years of memorable service.

MacKinnon had completed his contract at Firhill and was up-for-grabs. Greig didn't hesitate and he says: "That was £30,000 well spent. The lad has never let us down.

"He shows the determination, character and will-to-win that I like to see in all my players."

The raiding right-back became an instant hit with the Ibrox following with his timely tackling and lung-bursting surges down the wing to attack retreating rearguards.

Suddenly, MacKinnon, after years of being on the receiving end with clubs such as Dundee and Partick Thistle, was seeing football through the eyes of an Old Firm player and he admits: "I was revelling in that atmosphere.

'INCREDIBLE'

"But I got used to big crowds when I was a teenager with Arsenal and we went on a trip to Iran. Crowds of around 100,000 turned up to watch us in action in a Youth tournament. It was incredible, really.

"Players such as Liam Brady, Frank Stapleton and David O'Leary were with Arsenal at the time, but things didn't work out for me at Highbury and I was happy to return to Scotland."

MacKinnon's unpredictable career has ridden the big dipper of soccer fortunes, but he points out emphatically: "At last I've arrived and I'm really enjoying my football at Ibrox.

"I'll never admit I'm a first team regular in this company. I'm just taking every game as it comes. Every game is a bonus."

After all, according to one sports reporter, MacKinnon's career ended over two years ago . . .

WHAT STANDARD OF FOOTBALL DID YOU PLAY?

I am afraid I was only a run-of-the-mill full-back in a local Sheffield League. I did not win any honours although I was captain of Broomhill Sports.

WHEN DID YOU FIRST BECOME INTERESTED IN REFEREEING?

By mistake, really. I was playing for Broomhill when someone suggested that one of the players should go on a course to learn the Laws of the Game. It was 1960, and I was so interested that I decided to drop football and turn my sights to refereeing. One of my first matches involved Sheffield United juniors and I even had to borrow some kit from a friend.

WERE THERE TIMES WHEN YOU FELT LIKE PACKING IT IN?

Never. I've had rough patches like any player but I can assure you that finishing has never entered my mind. I love the game.

REF

KEITH HACKETT, one of the League's top officials and SHOOT's resident referee, answers some searching questions about his interesting career.

Keith in charge of the 1981 F.A. Cup Final replay between Spurs and Man. City.

WHY DID YOU MAKE IT WHEN SO MANY FAIL?

Two essential attributes are application and dedication – and fortunately I have them. When I first started I used to referee over 100 games a season and I was always disappointed when the campaign finished because I could never get enough of football. And I think that is why I eventually made it to the Football League.

BIGGGEST PROBLEM WHEN YOU GOT ON THE LIST?

I was fortunate to serve my apprenticeship in the Northern Premier League. There the standard is high and it prepares you for the step-up to the Football League. I had been a ref for 10 or 11 years so I had a lot of experience behind me and once I reached the physical level I had no problems. I started as a linesman and learnt everything by watching the likes of Jack Taylor and Clive Thomas in action. I picked up a lot of useful tips.

WHAT IS YOUR MOST AMUSING INCIDENT?

I believe there's a lot of fun in football. One incident that sticks out in my mind happened during my early career as the man in the middle. I refereed a

meant I returned there the following Thursday. I must admit the second game was superb, especially Ricky Villa's winner for Spurs.

WHO IS THE GREATEST PLAYER YOU HAVE BEEN IN CHARGE OF?

I have been privileged to have refereed Liverpool on a few occasions. And the one player I marvel at is Kenny Dalglish. The Scottish international is brilliant and possesses unbelievable skills. I was also fortunate enough to be a linesman with Bobby Charlton and Denis Law in the same Manchester United line-up.

WHAT ADVICE WOULD YOU GIVE TO ANY WOULD-BE REFEREES?

You must be dedicated. Set targets within your reach. If, for instance, you are a Class Three ref, then say to yourself I want to be a Class One official. Don't think about refereeing the F.A. Cup Final but just take each step as it comes. It's a marvellous opportunity to travel the world and to meet thousands of people. I've certainly been fortunate but I have also worked hard to get any rewards that I achieve and with the same sort of dedication anything is possible. Good Luck.

ON THE SPOT

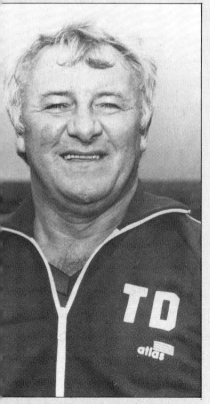
Man. United manager Tommy Docherty praised Keith's handling of a certain game. But certain fans thought otherwise!

Sunderland v Manchester United game and was in the bath afterwards, listening to the sports reports on the radio. United manager Tommy Docherty said that I had a great game even though his side had lost 2-1. You can imagine how I felt, I was on cloud nine. As I was leaving Roker Park, a young fan came up to me and asked for my autograph. After searching for pen and paper I duly signed it. The kid took one look at it, tore it up and said: "My Dad thinks you're rubbish!" That brought me down to earth with a bang. But I had a good laugh later.

THE HARDEST GAME YOU HAVE REFEREED?

Believe it or not it was between Stafford Rangers and Boston United. Boston were winning 3-1 when all hell broke loose after an off-the-ball incident which I and my linesman had not seen. A Stafford player was on the ground with deep facial cuts. It was very difficult to keep the game flowing after that because I was suspicious of every player. I and my officials needed a police escort off the pitch at the end. A very unpleasant experience.

YOUR MOST MEMORABLE?

The 100th F.A. Cup Final between Tottenham and Manchester City. It must be every League referee's dream to officiate the highlight of the season. It was another bonus for me when the game went to a replay because it

Keith is a great admirer of Liverpool star Kenny Dalglish.

David has brawn as well as brains. Here, as a West Ham player, he shields the ball from Manchester United's tough-tackling Gordon McQueen in the 1980 F.A. Cup Final.

'I'M GETTING WISER'

admits David Cross, the soccer academic

The Legal profession's loss was Soccer's gain when David Cross elected to turn down the University place offered to him to study law and instead took up a career in football with Rochdale.

He stayed with them from the age of 18 until he was 22, was then transferred to Norwich after which he started on a short series of moves while scoring regularly for each of his clubs. After two years with Norwich it was on to Coventry for three years, West Bromwich Albion for one year, West Ham for five years and then on to Manchester City.

Does he think it was a wise move to choose Soccer and would he recommend any lad to embrace a career in the game?

"Yes," he answers without hesitation, "I do not regret my decision. It is a great way to earn a living because you really love what you are doing. But it is a much harder job than most people either imagine or realise.

"Many think we are only involved on a Saturday when we play matches because they tend to regard the game as only being played on Saturday afternoon. They do not think that we play two matches a week throughout most of the season and train hard during the rest of the week.

"The season is long and hard, but anyone with talent should not be afraid to take the chance.

"When I went to West Ham, I was approaching maturity as a player and was ready to learn new things. I feel I played far better than at any previous time in my career. Now I expect to improve even more over the next few years because I'm getting wiser.

"I have pushed up my goal ratio in that time from one goal in three matches to one goal in two, and whilst some people are saying that the quality of some of my goals is improving that does not really matter much, although it is rather pleasing.

"It does not matter how you score the goals as long as you score them, since I feel I am not paid to score only 'good' goals, and they all count.

"Most clubs nowadays tend to play with two central strikers and they must work for one another. Goals come from chances created and I think there is a direct ratio between the number of chances created and the number of goals scored."

David has many interests off the field. He says jokingly: "The image I do not want to convey is that I am a person who just goes home from training, plays a game of golf, reads, does a crossword, listens to some music and then goes to bed. Whilst I like to be serious and read books, which I think helps self-education and takes away the tedium of long coach and train journeys, I still like to enjoy the lively side of life.

"I have had some wonderful moments, including being in West Ham's Cup-Winning side in 1980, which was the highlight of my playing days so far, because it gave immense pleasure to my family and friends. Then we returned to Wembley twice more in less than twelve months with the Charity Shield and the League Cup Final. I also enjoyed our short stint in Europe where I scored in every Round we played in and I got a hat-trick in one match played behind locked doors."

Although David went to play in the North American Soccer League last summer, one day he could again be thrilling English crowds!

Who would have believed that a 40-year-old would lift the World Cup in triumph? Aren't footballers meant to be over the hill at 30? Dino Zoff is a name for the annals of football. He's seen it all during over two decades of first-class action. He's been adored. He's been hated. He's been voted the best. He's

First Round by Poland and Argentina – and a great goal by Haiti striker Sanon put an end to an unbelievable performance by Zoff. He'd been unbeaten in the Italian goal for 1,070 minutes.

Four years later, in Argentina, Zoff was the great scapegoat as Italy returned home with a creditable fourth place. In 1974, the entire squad had been pelted with tomatoes at the airport, but this time most of the rotten fruit went Dino's way, with critics blaming him for the two Dutch goals that cost Enzo Bearzot's team a place in the Final.

Finally, in Spain in 1982, at the fourth attempt, Zoff's dream came true.

"I can only thank God for all the

watched replays of the goal hundreds of time, and I still believe that shot was unstoppable.

"Any goalkeeper has to expect criticism, because practically all your mistakes are goals. Young goalkeepers have to accept this as part of the job.

"People started asking me when I was going to retire way back in 1967 when I was 25! Although I pulled out of international football following the defeat in Rumania that wrecked our hopes of qualifying for next year's European Championships, I still plan to continue to serve my club. I don't care if I am called 'Dino the Dinosaur'"

GRANDAD ZOFF
Life doesn't end at forty

been written off as a no-hoper. He's been quoted as an example of eternal youth. And he's been rated so old and crochety that they've called him Dino the Dinosaur . . .

The Zoff story started on February 28th 1942, and his professional debut came 19 years later with just four appearances between the posts for relegation-bound Udinese. In 1963, after a year in the Second Division, he moved to Mantova, where he once again savoured the pleasures of relegation before moving on to Napoli in 1967. Five years later, he was signed by Juventus, and went on to establish an amazing record of missing only seven games (in the 1971-72 season) in 18 years.

And who would have thought that when he signed for Juventus at the age of 30, he would still have time to pick up five League medals; and several major Cups. Life begins at 30!

Meanwhile, Zoff's international career had begun in 1968 and en route to breaking Facchetti's record of 94 Italian caps and joining the tiny elite who've won more than a hundred, Dino's travels included four World Cups. In Mexico in 1970, he sat on the sidelines as reserve to Albertosi. In 1974, in West Germany, Italy were bumped out of the competition in the

good fortune he's given me over the years, and for this fine reward.

"There's no secret behind my performance. I don't think 40 is old for a goalkeeper, anyway. I have simply dedicated my whole life to football – I don't regard it as 'work', it's more like a hobby.

"I recognise that I've been spared serious injuries, and I feel tremendous sympathy for people like Gordon Banks who are forced prematurely out of the game by injuries. For me, he was the best goalkeeper of all time.

"The other thing I've had to do over the years is to grow a skin as thick as an elephant's. I've had to put up with some brutal criticism over the years, and even after our World Cup win in 1982, someone said on TV that it had been no thanks to me.

"But 1978 was a lot worse. Even the Press started calling me Blindman Zoff because I let in that 30-metre shot from Haan in the Holland game. I've

Quicksilver wingers, brilliant goalkeepers, mean defenders, inspired midfield players – they all begin their football lives in school, youth and park teams.

Millions of boys dream of being spotted by a scout or manager and becoming a professional player. Every year another batch disappear behind the doors of the 92 League clubs, knowing that even their select numbers will be whittled down inside a couple of

seasons. A heartbreaking experience

Countless boys will tell you that they failed to make the grade at clubs where less skilful lads were kept on. Others complain that they were the strongest or fittest candidates but were eventually released while skinnier characters, some with spectacles, were signed.

The question so often asked is: "What does a manager look for in a potential player? Is

TO BE A STAR, MANAGERS ALL AGREE, YOU'VE GOT TO HAVE S-K

Steve McMahon's superb fitness proves his manager's point.

"Finally I want to see boys with the courage to fail! As a striker I believed that I needed the courage to miss before I would become a consistent scorer. By this I mean the guts to have a go, the guts to play the difficult pass, attempt the painful tackle, risk the header that could break your nose or win the game."

Scotland winger Eddie Gray, who won 12 caps for his country during a

'A lad's physical condition plays an important part'
Howard Kendall (Everton)

'He must have confidence in his own ability'
Malcolm Macdonald (Fulham)

against the odds and make other people play?

"I believe the boy's background is important, the stability of his life and his way of life.

"Then I assess his overall potential. I watch his contribution over 90 minutes and how he reacts to physical contact, frustration, knocks and criticism. Put all these together and it's a comprehensive examination."

Macdonald, manager of Fulham, the club with whom he began his League career, has 14 England caps that sum up his impressive pedigree.

"I look for self belief, the confidence in his own ability that takes him above the rest. Then I look for attitude, the character in the boy and his will to succeed and be a winner.

"Dedication to the game is important, although this is something you assess better after getting to know a player. But there are tell-tale signs from the start.

"You must include the skill factor. A player aiming for the professional game must have a degree of natural skill. It may be an individual strength such as heading, shooting power, tackling bite or whatever. But that basic skill must be there in the first place.

Everton manager Kendall, who won the League Championship with Everton and played in two F.A. Cup Finals, said: "A lad's physical condition plays an important part, not because players need to be muscle-bound, but it is important if a boy has the overall strength to compete.

"The skill-factor is very important. Naturally you expect the player to have a level of skill in the first place. But you have to assess the degree of skill in relation to where he plays and his reactions under pressure.

"The attitude is very important. Does the boy want to be a winner? Does he have the character to fight

Gordon Davies could not score so many goals if he was not sure of his ability.

106

there a common denominator such as strength, skill, discipline or ambition that appears repeatedly on the assessment sheets of the 92 League bosses?"

We selected four top managers at random and asked them to list their five most important pointers when they are watching a player for the first time. And all four included one 'Common Denominator' . . . skill!

All four men – Malcolm Macdonald, Howard Kendall, Ken Brown and Eddie Gray – can boast sparkling playing careers. All played in the First Division, three of them for their countries and all won medals at the highest level. So they know exactly what it takes to not only make the grade but become professional stars.

Each manager had different priorities and some included factors that others did not. But all four included . . . skill!

Mark Barham is regarded as a great prospect at Carrow Road.

Aiden Butterworth exemplifies his manager's basic belief.

'Character also plays an important part in the making of a player'
Ken Brown (Norwich)

'If you cannot control a ball and pass it, you can't play'
Eddie Gray (Leeds)

glorious career with Leeds United, is now manager at Elland Road. And he puts the skill factor top of his list.

"As Bill Shankly said, 'If you cannot control a ball and pass it, you cannot play.' It seems harsh but it's a fact.

"I look for these two skills in any outfield player. Some have strengths to add or even compensate for lesser degrees of skill, but the skill must be there to start with.

"Billy Bremner and John Giles were competitors; men who could tackle and win battles for you when the chips were down. But just recall their immense skills on the ball as well. Need I say more?

"I look for the physical aspects as well. I expect a centre-forward, for example, to have a degree of strength and determination as well as skill.

Some lads develop too soon and are 'burnt out' compared with other lads of their age. Others begin slowly, look a bit raw but have the rough edges worth smoothing. They can blossom in their late teens and go on to be stars."

Norwich manager and former England defender Ken Brown says: "I go for the basic skill factor. I look for the boy who can control the ball in any situation and pass it accurately. These may seem obvious points but they are also the basics of our game.

"Next comes his attitude and will to be the best in the business. I expect players to seek excellence at their job.

"Character plays an important part in the making of a player because it is not enough to possess a god-given skill without having the inner drive to

make it pay and work for you.

"I look for small tell-tale things, albeit most of which reveal themselves after a lad has been in your club for a while. Temperament, attitude to losing and ability to cope with praise and criticism.

"I like a player to be positive and a person willing to exhibit his own skills while also being part of a team unit."

Four managers who have bought and sold stars. Four men who have earned the game's top awards on the strength of their playing ability. All four know what they want to see in the player of tomorrow. Their common denominator is SKILL.

Mickey settled at City

Just the mention of season 1981-82 is enough to make Mickey Thomas turn white. Like a recurring nightmare it haunts the Welsh international winger's private moments as he recalls how close his career came to falling apart.

Life was sweet for the hard-working little Mochdre-born winger when he operated the full length of Manchester United's left flank under Dave Sexton's management.

The Old Trafford fans took workaholic Thomas to their hearts as United finished runners-up to Liverpool in the First Division in 1980, 12 months after failing in the dying seconds against Arsenal in the F.A. Cup Final.

But Sexton's departure spelt the end also for Thomas who was transferred to Everton in 1981.

"That's when my problems began. I could not settle down at Goodison and after only 10 League appearances, without scoring a goal, I was transferred again, down to Brighton.

"But although I tried I could not work it out in Sussex. It was too far from home and my heart belonged further north.

LOST SEASON

"It was a rough time because my form suffered and my international career seemed to suffer as well. I could hardly blame Mike England for putting me in and out of the side, sometimes as sub.

"Then Ritchie Barker stepped in and since joining Stoke, and linking up again with my former United mate Sammy McIlroy, my career has taken off again. In 20 League outings for Brighton I also failed to find the net, yet I quickly put that right at Stoke.

"It's all a matter of being settled in your mind and confident about your game. And once I'd put that awful season behind me — almost a lost season in my career — I re-established myself with Wales and that was always of tremendous importance to me.

"I'm fiercely proud of that red jersey and love my homeland. Yet already I seem to be an adopted Midlander."

What about the future? "I want to help Stoke win a major honour. Ritchie Barker has built an exciting, attacking team at the Victoria Ground and we play just the type of football I love. Hopefully I can repay his faith in me in that way."

West Ham star Paul Goddard would rather create goals than score them. That may seem strange coming from a top striker who aims to be a member of the England team competing in the next World Cup Finals.

"I know it's odd for a recognised striker to say that, but I mean it," says Paul. "I honestly believe there's more to my game than just scoring goals.

"Most strikers aren't happy unless they are knocking them in week after week, no matter how well they are playing.

"I'm different. Scoring goals is not enough for me. I must feel as though I'm making a contribution to the team in other ways, like making chances for a front-running partner.

"As long as I'm maintaining a high level of consistent form I'm happy. Goals come second."

travels daily to West Ham's training ground at Chadwell Heath in Essex.

"It's a long way, but all my family and friends are in that area. Anyway it's not so bad because I travel in with West Ham's other West London commuters Phil Parkes and Alan Devonshire.

"As soon as I get home I forget all about football, though. It's a job of work to me and I like to shut off completely and talk about other things."

Does that suggest that perhaps Paul hasn't the ambition to go right to the top?

"Nonsense," he says with just a

moment of almost apologetic anger.

"I want to be a success with England and help them win the World Cup in 1986. I desperately want West Ham to win the Championship. The whole game would benefit if a team with manager John Lyall's ideals won the title."

The game would also be a great deal richer with players of Paul's character.

"How right you are," agrees John Lyall.

"Paul is the sort of lad who will go through his career without giving a moment of trouble to his club or manager."

Sarge has certainly earned his stripes . . . a tremendous example to all youngsters when he's on parade for The Hammers and England.

'SARGE' HAS EARNED HIS STRIPES

Goddard, signed from Q.P.R. for a West Ham record £800,000 fee in August, 1980, is one of soccer's unlikeliest stars.

Clean-cut, quietly spoken, Paul looks more like a rising young City executive than a trendy professional footballer.

He shuns the glamour and has no time for the rich hangers on who latch on to players like gold-plated leeches.

His parents are practising Baptists so Paul has been brought up to respect other people and understand the need for discipline and self-control.

"Naturally I sometimes get annoyed when I'm hacked down. But I just walk away.

"My attitude upsets my wife Debbie who says I should hit back. But that's not my way, even though the pressures and stress have increased in the game."

Paul's years in the Boys Brigade, rising to the rank of Warrant Officer, gave him a good grounding and outlook on life.

"The B.B. keeps kids off the streets and teaches them to mix with other races. There's a uniform and a bit of drill, so it gives them a sense of unity and discipline."

When Paul was taking and making goals for Clive Allen at Q.P.R. he was active in the Brigade as a sergeant.

Johnny Hollins was also at Loftus Road at the time and gave Paul the nickname "Sarge". He's still called that by his West Ham team-mates.

Paul lives with Debbie in a detached house near Uxbridge, Middlesex and

Throughout his ten years at the top, Kevin Keegan's life on and off the pitch has been charted in our newspapers, and on radio and TV. His bubbling personality and all-action style have gained him millions of fans throughout the football world. But in how much detail do you recall his fabulous career? From the moment he joined Liverpool, where devoted Kopites christened him "Mighty Mouse", to his signing by Newcastle United.

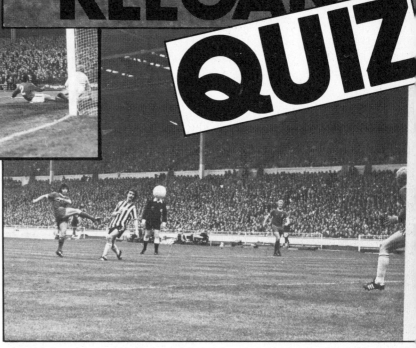

THE KEVIN KEEGAN QUIZ

No great scholar at school, Kevin had only one thought in his mind: to become a professional footballer. Despite being rejected as too small by a certain Midlands club, he persevered in his ambition and was rewarded with a place at a seaside club (right). **(1) Name the club that signed him. (2) Which club rejected him: West Bromwich Albion, Coventry City or Birmingham City? (3) Know his birthday – it falls on a certain day in February?**

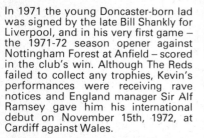

In 1971 the young Doncaster-born lad was signed by the late Bill Shankly for Liverpool, and in his very first game – the 1971-72 season opener against Nottingham Forest at Anfield – scored in the club's win. Although The Reds failed to collect any trophies, Kevin's performances were receiving rave notices and England manager Sir Alf Ramsey gave him his international debut on November 15th, 1972, at Cardiff against Wales.

(4) England won 1-0. Did Kevin (centre) score the goal? (5) Another Liverpool player made his debut that day – was it Ray Clemence, Emlyn Hughes or Ian Callaghan?

The end of the 1972-73 season saw Kevin collect his first two major honours. One for the League Championship, which Liverpool won with 60 points, three points more than Arsenal in second place. And the other medal for helping Liverpool win the U.E.F.A. Cup for the very first time. At the end of the second-leg joyful fans paid tribute to his contribution to the game by chairing him shoulder-high from the pitch (left).

(6) Name the West German side Liverpool defeated – Bayern Munich, Borussia Moenchengladbach or Cologne?

1974 was a year of ecstasy and agony for Kevin. In the F.A. Cup Final at Wembley Liverpool humbled the club he was later to join – those great Cup-fighters Newcastle United – by 3-0. But his world crashed during the Charity Shield curtain-raiser at Wembley between the F.A. Cup winners and League Champions Leeds United. He suffered the terrible humiliation of being sent off, along with United's captain, for a sudden flare-up between them.

(7) How many goals did Kevin score in the Final? (8) Who was United's captain?

In 1976, Kevin starred in another fabulous double win – the Championship and a second U.E.F.A. Cup, this time over Belgian club Bruges. (He's celebrating the occasion with team-mates). To crown his season he was voted Footballer of the Year, and presented with the trophy by a former great Everton goalscorer.

(9) In the second-leg of the U.E.F.A. Final, in Bruges, Liverpool were trailing 1-0, but Kevin scored the goal that levelled the score and won the Cup. How did he score that goal? (10) Name the legendary figure with Kevin in the presentation photo below.

The highspot of Kevin's career with Liverpool came in 1977 – the European Cup Final against the team they had beaten to the 1973 U.E.F.A. Cup, Borussia Moenchengladbach. It was a June night to remember, as tens of thousands of Liverpool supporters descended on Rome in expectation of their team's first-ever European Cup win. Their favourites did not disappoint them. In one of the most thrilling Finals ever in this competition, they ran out 3-1 winners. Kevin is shown waving to the fans in the company of his friend Dave Johnson, a substitute on the great occasion.

(11) What other honours did Kevin win at the end of that season? (12) What part did Kevin play in Liverpool's third goal?

In need of a new challenge, Kevin succeeded in obtaining a transfer to West Germany's Hamburg SV. At first he found the transition difficult. Many of the team resented him. It was then that his strong character emerged. Refusing to quit, he stuck to his task and a new team was built around him.

(13) Hamburg paid £600,000 or £700,000 for his services? (14) He played against his old club Liverpool for the Super Cup and Hamburg lost by what score on aggregate?

Thanks to Kevin's efforts, Hamburg won the West German Championship in 1979, which qualified them for the European Cup the following season. Unfortunately his dreams of winning a second winner's medal were wrecked by an English team in the Final in Madrid, Spain, (above) before a crowd of 50,000.

(15) Who were Hamburg's opponents and what was the score?

At this time Kevin was probably playing the best football of his career. He had added a new dimension to his game, the ability to deal with man to man marking. Narrowly beaten in the poll for the 1977 European Player of the Year award – the vote went to Allan Simonsen, who last season had a short spell with Charlton Athletic – he won it in 1978.

(16) Did he win it again the following year, 1979?

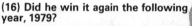

THE KEVIN KEEGAN QUIZ

In 1980 Kevin decided he wished to return to English football. Not to join one of the acknowledged great clubs, such as Liverpool or Manchester United, but to take his talents to unfashionable Southampton. Here he's at the signing-on ceremony with his wife Jean, daughter Laura-Jane and Saints' manager Lawrie McMenemy and wife Pat.

(17) What fee did Southampton pay – £400,000, £500,000 or £600,000?

Even while in Germany, Kevin had continued to play for England, often enduring long and uncomfortable journeys to join-up with his team-mates. He dedicated himself to leading England into the 1982 World Cup Finals. As captain, he was a marvellous leader and inspired his team to several fine wins. The most crucial was the game against Hungary at Wembley in November, 1982, (above) when he was once again captain.

(18) England won – by what score?

Kevin has always had a knack of springing surprises, and he lived up to his reputation by deciding to leave Southampton – where he was as popular as he'd been with his previous clubs – and accept a new challenge at Newcastle. In one of his early League matches (below) he scored four goals, including one penalty – in Newcastle's 5-1 win over Rotherham, player-managed by his one-time Liverpool team-mate Emlyn Hughes.

(19) What was his transfer fee from Southampton – £100,000, £180,000 or £220,000?

In November, 1982, Kevin joined the ranks of the footballers honoured by the Queen for their services to football. Accompanied by his wife Jean and elder daughter Laura-Jane – his second was too young to attend – he went to Buckingham Palace for his investiture.

(20) Did he receive the MBE or the OBE?

Another memento for him to treasure. For us, we are content with the memory of a man who gives everything – in every game!

ANSWERS

(1) Scunthorpe United.
(2) Coventry City.
(3) February 14th – St. Valentine's Day.
(4) No – Colin Bell.
(5) Ray Clemence.
(6) Borussia Moenchengladbach.
(7) Two – he is shown scoring his first.
(8) Billy Bremner.
(9) From a free-kick.
(10) The late Dixie Dean.
(11) The League Championship and F.A. Cup losers' medal.
(12) He was brought down by Borussia's Berti Vogts in the penalty area, and Phil Neal scored from the resulting penalty kick.
(13) £700,000.
(14) 7-1.
(15) Nottingham Forest, 1-0. Goal scored by John Robertson.
(16) Yes.
(17) £400,000.
(18) 1-0. Goal scored by Paul Mariner.
(19) £100,000.
(20) OBE.

"FANS AFFECT MY GAME"

JOHN ROBERTSON

John Robertson, a European Cup winner, League Champion and Football League Cup winner with Nottingham Forest, has a heart-felt message to football fans the world over: "Never, ever under-estimate your influence on the players you support."

The Scotland World Cup winger surprised many of his fellow professionals when he admitted that criticism from the terraces has, and still does, affect his form.

Robertson has overcome a number of problems during his career, not the least of which was a long-running disagreement with former Forest assistant manager Peter Taylor.

It was Taylor, then Brian Clough's partner, who rounded on Robertson, called him an overweight park player and helped the talented Scot to become an international class winger.

Yet it's the fans who have the biggest influence on Robertson. "I've been 15 years with the same club and I admit there was a time when I was very keen for a change.

ROUGH TIME

"Maybe the fans sense as much because I began to get a lot of stick from the terraces. It really got through to me, even after all these years in the game.

"I doubt if many fans know how much they can affect a player's game by giving him a rough time as an individual. It's bad enough when the whole team gets the bird but when the supporters decided to single out one player it can make his life a hell. Some lads in the League admit that they have preferred playing in away games!

"The Forest fans have, by and large, been very good to me. And I like to think I've given reasonable value for their money. It is just that I believe it's about time I held up my hands and admitted that when they have a go, yes, it does hit home."

But does it have a positive influence or does it make things worse?

"That depends on the player. I only know that it makes me worry and also makes me rethink how I am playing. I suppose that has its good sides. But I definitely prefer it when the fans are behind me. Then I know I can give my best."

Surely the sentiment of every professional in the game. Fans take note!

CHRIS IS AIMING HIGH!

There's nothing unusual about a Londoner playing for Tottenham Hotspur. But there is when a West Ham born lad also turns out for the Republic of Ireland. Chris Hughton, who qualifies under the parentage ruling, has no regrets about missing out on the chance to play for England. He's as fanatical about playing for the Emerald Isle as he is for the club at White Hart Lane. One of his biggest disappointments was missing out on the 1982 World Cup, but he's hoping to wipe that out by helping his country to qualify for the 1984 European Championships in France. Strangely, for an attack-minded full-back he feels his country would benefit from adopting caution as its watchword. "We tend to be too adventurous," he says, "For instance, when we played Spain in

Dublin in our opening match we attacked without care and paid the penalty by going 1–3 down. We were fortunate to peg two goals back.

Chris is still optimistic about the Republic's chances. "We have the ability to pull off some surprises. Just like Northern Ireland did in the World Cup in Spain."

Apart from his international ambitions, Chris wants to win more silverware with Spurs. He signed as a part-timer for them in June 1977, and turned full professional two years later. And within another two years he was the proud owner of two F.A. Cup medals. Chris is a quality player destined for even greater things. He expects to go up in the world. Not surprising in a lad who has also qualified as a lift engineer!

NOT ONLY WITH SPURS, BUT WITH THE REPUBLIC OF IRELAND

OVERNIGHT SUCCESS

DAVID NAREY is the Scottish international star with a remarkable claim to fame . . .

He became an overnight success after being involved in the international arena for FIVE years!

When the super-cool Dundee United star strode confidently onto a headed pass by John Wark to unleash a shot of superb quality and precision behind the helpless Brazilian goalkeeper Waldir Peres during the epic World Cup encounter in Spain suddenly his name was on the lips of everyone.

"Yes, I'll always remember that goal," says Narey. "It's just a pity that we could not hold that lead against the Brazilians.

"They came straight back at us, of course, and eventually we went down 4–1. Still, it was nice to score that goal."

Jock Stein pays tribute to the professionalism of non-nonsense Narey, a dedicated club player who has shown no inclination to try his luck across the Border.

"I recall a game where I had 17 players available for selection," says the Scots supremo. "That meant I would be naming my line-up with five substitutes and one player not getting stripped at all.

"At that time it was David Narey who was not involved. He accepted my judgement and I was impressed by his attitude."

Narey has played right-back, sweeper, central defence and midfield for Scotland. Which position does he prefer?

He answers: "I suppose I'm at my happiest in the middle of the back-four, but I'll always do my best no matter where I'm told to play.

"I much prefer the play coming towards me with the chance to break into attack whenever I think something is on."

It was from such an opening that Narey scored his breathtaking goal against the Brazilians in Seville in '82.

As Graeme Souness and Asa Hartford dwelt on the ball on the left, Narey expertly moved forward. Souness swept over a cross any Brazilian would be proud of and John Wark was there to nod it down.

Narey burst forward, tamed the ball and then unleashed a shot of awesome power high into the net. It was rated one of the finest goals of the World Cup Finals even though TV pundit Jimmy Hill called it a "toe-poke".

Although Narey will never be famous for the amount of goals he scores, he does tend to hit spectacular efforts.

He scored another magnificent goal in last season's UEFA Cup Third Round tie against West Germany's Werder Bremen when he chipped a 25-yard free-kick over the head of goalkeeper Burdenski to help his side into the Quarter-Finals on a 3–2 aggregate.

But what is quiet man Narey's proudest moment? He says: "When I made my international debut against Sweden at Hampden. I was the first-ever Dundee United player to win a full cap."

Share with England and Liverpool defender Phil Thompson his memories of those unforgettable first-time moments . . .

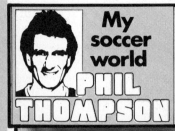

My soccer world PHIL THOMPSON

"FABULOUS NIGHT"

I was born in Merseyside, and the first words my mother taught me were "Liverpool F.C." She was a fanatic – still is! – but my Dad was then an Everton supporter, so just Mum and I and my brother went to Anfield to cheer on The Reds. I'll never forget the first big game she took me to – it was in 1965, the first leg of the European Cup Semi-Final against the Italian Champions Inter-Milan. What a fabulous night. The F.A. Cup, which Liverpool had won the previous year by beating Leeds United, was on show, and my favourites beat the Italians by 3-1. My particular heroes – Ian St. John, Ian Callaghan and Roger Hunt – each scored a goal!

FIFTY FANS

My first game as a Liverpool player took place in front of 50 fans – not at Anfield but at Melwood, the training ground. I was 13 at the time, playing for the "B" team against Bury. The pouring rain failed to dampen my spirits. I was realising my greatest ambition – to play in that famous red shirt!

BEATING BEST

My first run-out with the first team was as a sub. at Old Trafford against a Manchester United packed with great names. We were winning 2-0 when I came on. I got my first touch

'FIRSTS'!

when George Best tried to "nutmeg" me — attempted to push the ball between my legs. I shook my knees, trapped the ball, and it was George, not me, who ended up with the red face! My first full game came soon after, against Norwich City.

MY RECORD

In 1973, I won my first honour with the club. A League Championship medal, which I collected at a banquet. I've gone on to add several more to that particular collection. In fact, I've won more Championship medals with the same club than any other player!

GLORIOUS GOAL

Thompson goals are almost as rare as an Evertonian standing at the Kop end of Anfield, so I can remember every one I've scored. The first time I appeared on the Liverpool scoresheet was after a 2-0 win over Derby County in 1973 at Anfield. The ball came over from a corner; I closed my eyes and lashed at it. When I opened them it was to see the ball screaming into the net. Kevin Keegan has never stopped ribbing me about it!

F.A. CUP MEDAL

It's well-known that every player's ambition is to play at Wembley and win the F.A. Cup. It first happened to me in 1974, and I still rate the experience as amongst my best ever. We were playing Newcastle United, those mighty Cup fighters, and the general opinion was that they would win. I remember one newspaper saying that the United strike force of Malcolm Macdonald and John Tudor had too much experience for a lad like me. Which really wound me up, and I was pleased to ram the writer's words down his throat by helping us win 3-0 in a really one-sided Final. Incidentally, one of United's players, Terry McDermott, later transferred to Liverpool and became one of my biggest mates.

ENGLAND DEBUT

Almost two years later I had my first game for England, making my debut alongside two other Liverpool lads, Phil Neal and Ray Kennedy. It wasn't an easy baptism. I found myself up against a big, bustling, former Arsenal player named John Roberts. But we came away from Wrexham with a 2-1 win. It was even more memorable for Ray. He scored one of our goals.

"FOREIGN" MEDAL

And it was in the same year, 1976, I won my first European medal, following a narrow U.E.F.A. Cup win on aggregate over Bruges, a strong Belgian team. We only beat them 3-2 at Anfield, and when they went one-up from a penalty conversion after Tommy Smith had handled in our penalty area, things looked dicey. But then Kevin Keegan scored from a free-kick and the trophy was ours!

BIG MOMENT

My first England goal was scored in America! We were over there in 1976 to play in a tournament commemorating their bi-centenary. Italy were one of our opponents, and on a terrible pitch — one quarter was not grass but the clay part of a baseball

diamond — we found ourselves 2-0 down within 20 minutes. But Mick Channon scored, and then my big moment arrived. The ball came over from a corner and bounced in front of keeper Dino Zoff, who took his eyes off it, distracted by the sight of big Joe Royle coming at him like an express train. I took advantage and drove the ball home. Mick scored a second goal to give us a 3-2 win!

LEADING ENGLAND

Another unforgettable "first" for me was leading England out against Bulgaria in November 1979. I was standing in for Kevin Keegan. The game had been scheduled for the previous evening, but had to be called off due to thick fog at Wembley. And as Kevin was recalled by Hamburg SV to prepare for a vital weekend match, the then-manager Ron Greenwood turned to me and said: "You're captain of Liverpool the League leaders. You couldn't be better qualified." A marvellous honour for me, especially as we came off 2-0 winners!

NEAR MISS

Playing in a World Cup Finals is the dream of all players. Mine came true in 1982 in Spain. We got off to a terrific start with a 3-1 win over France, and my particular high spot was almost scoring with a 25-yard shot that just flew past the wrong side of a post. I've got my fingers crossed I'll play again in 1986 — and celebrate my first World Cup goal!

Far left: Phil celebrates his first goal for England. Left: Tackling Newcastle's John Tudor in Liverpool's 3-0 F.A. Cup Final victory in 1974. Right: In action against the host country in the 1982 World Cup Finals in Spain.

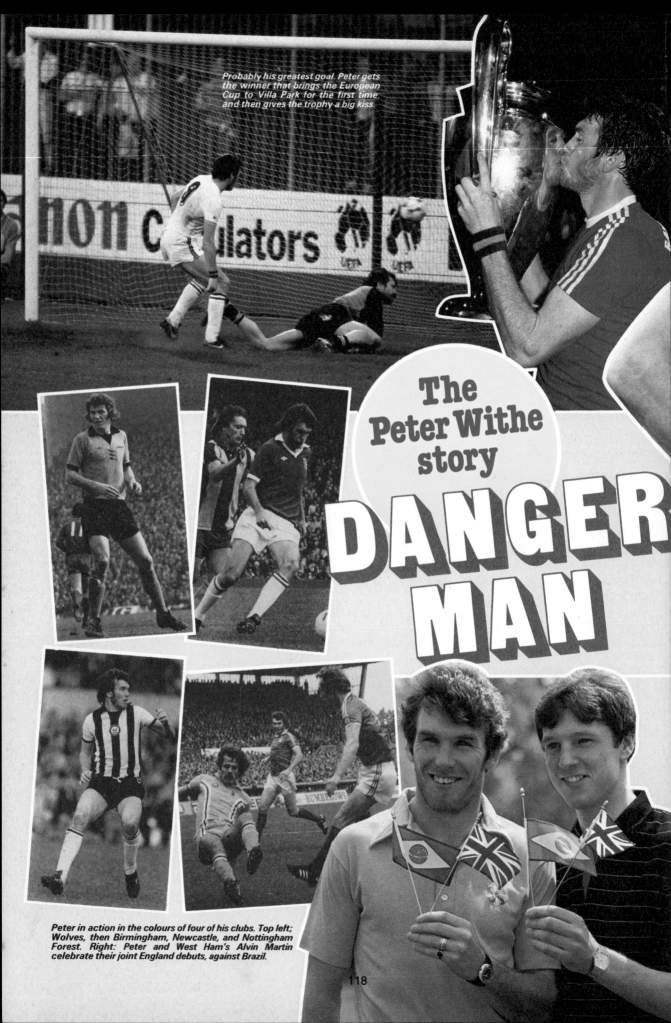

Probably his greatest goal. Peter gets the winner that brings the European Cup to Villa Park for the first time, and then gives the trophy a big kiss.

The Peter Withe story

DANGER MAN

Peter in action in the colours of four of his clubs. Top left; Wolves, then Birmingham, Newcastle, and Nottingham Forest. Right: Peter and West Ham's Alvin Martin celebrate their joint England debuts, against Brazil.

Celebrations after Villa won the League Championship in 1981. Peter and the other half of his scoring act, Gary Shaw.

first time in the club's history, the European Cup, when his goal – the only one of the European Cup Final against West Germany's Bayern Munich – secured the Continent's most prestigious trophy.

Peter has also won international recognition, being called to his country's colours in May, 1981. Unfortunately the opposition was Brazil, and although he played well in the friendly at Wembley, he failed to score and the mighty South Americans emerged as 1–0 winners.

Peter may never again win another cap – although the England manager is well aware he can always be counted upon – but on the club scene he will always be regarded as one of the most effective strikers to play alongside – and amongst the most deadly to face!

Below:
Proudly displaying the Midlands' Player of the Year trophy.

Ask centre-backs in England to make a short list of the strikers they rate as being hard to handle, and most are sure to include the name of Peter Withe. Peter may lack finesse, but his aggression and finishing power have singled him out as someone who will always end a season with a stack of goals to his credit. A much-travelled man, who began with non-League Southport, he has given value for money in terms of results to every club he has served. He first hit the headlines with Nottingham Forest under Brian Clough where he scored a total of 28 League goals in 75 appearances, helping them to the Championship in 1978. He also starred in the City Ground's first League Cup win that same year, when they beat Liverpool – after a replay.

The following season he was transferred to Second Division Newcastle United, who, despite all Peter's efforts, failed to win promotion. However, his ability had not gone unnoticed by Ron Saunders, then manager of Aston Villa, and he was signed for a club record fee of £500,000 in May 1980.

Perhaps his greatest period in football followed, as he helped Villa to win the League in 1981, and in 1982, for the

Above; Sharing the Charity Shield with Spurs' Mark Falco after Villa's 2–2 draw with the London club in 1981.

JEST THE JOB!

In the "Super Focus" feature in SHOOT magazine, players reveal the jobs they would have been doing if they hadn't gone into football. Our cartoonist decided to have fun with some answers . . .

JOCKEY —
Gordon McQueen (Manchester United)

SAFETY SUPERVISOR —
Neil Orr (West Ham)

DRIVING INSTRUCTOR —
John Wark (Ipswich)

CHARLIE NICHOLAS

Autograph: *[signature]*

Height: 5ft. 5-10ins

Weight: 11 stone

Birthday: December 30th

Birthplace: Glasgow.

Nickname: Nick or Charlie

First club: Celtic.

Favourite food: Prawn Cocktail.

Favourite drink: Lager

Favourite other sports: Golf & Snooker.

Most memorable match for (country): Under 21's Scotland v. Switzerland

Charlie (standing centre) watches in admiration as his team-mate, Richard Gough, scores Scotland's fourth goal in the win in Aarau.

Biggest disappointment: Breaking of my Leg.

Which person in the world would you most like to meet? The Next Marilyn Munroe

Most treasured football memento: Scotland's Young Player of the Year

Most memorable match at club level: League Cup Final Victory.

A near-miss for Charlie in Celtic's 2—1 win over Rangers in 1982. Although he did score his club's first goal.

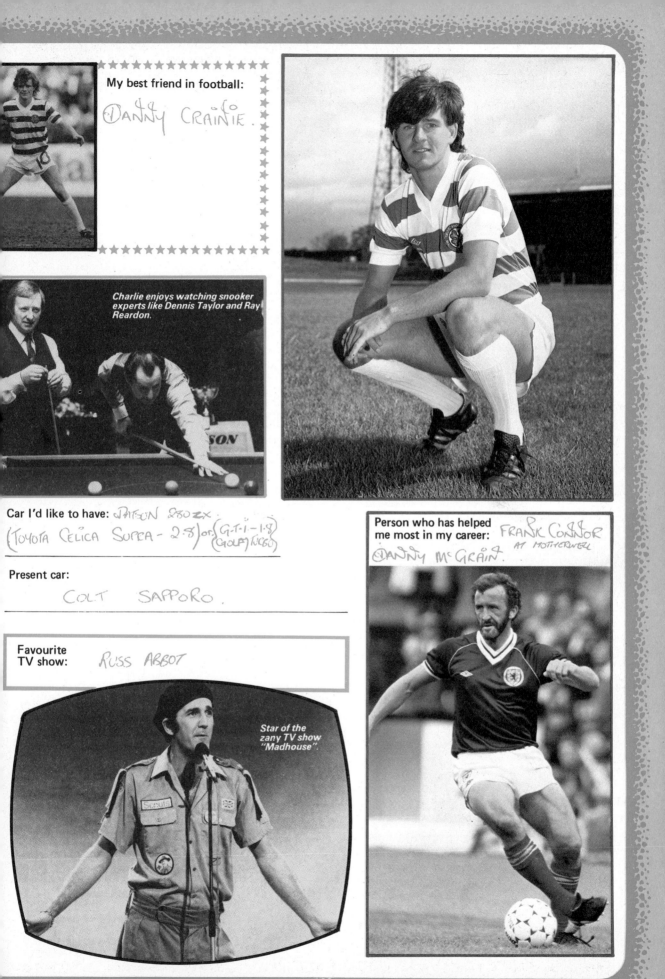

My best friend in football:

Danny Crainie.

Charlie enjoys watching snooker experts like Dennis Taylor and Ray Reardon.

Car I'd like to have: Datson 280 zx.
(Toyota Celica Supra - 2.8) or (G.T.i - 1.8)
(Golf Turbo)

Present car:

COLT SAPPORO.

Favourite TV show: Russ Abbot

Star of the zany TV show "Madhouse".

Person who has helped me most in my career: Frank Connor at Motherwell
Danny McGrain.

The F.A. Cup Final, surely the most famous knock-out cup competition in the world, is one long story of glory and heartache, magical moments and mysterious failures, inspiration, desperation and injury hoodoos.

Few Finals actually go the way the "experts" predict and many star players have stepped out of the tunnel, been singed by the heat of the Wembley roar and lost their nerve.

Equally, however, that astonishing and incomparable atmosphere generated by 100,000 people has had the reverse effect on players who, before the moment they first trod the famous turf, were far removed from the star status of many of their colleagues . . . yet ended the day local and national heroes.

Such has been the case throughout the history of the competition since its inception way back in 1871. Here we look at some of the post-War players who have become legends simply on the basis of their contribution to one game.

Ronnie Boyce was known as "Ticker" by his team mates because of his non-stop work in midfield. It was said that he made the likes of Peter Brabrook, Geoff Hurst, John Sissons and Johnny Byrne tick through 90 minutes.

But finishing was not one of Boyce's great strengths and therefore, as the gripping 1964 Cup Final edged into its closing stages, First Division Hammers were in grave danger of falling behind for the third time to Second Division Preston North End.

Sissons and Hurst had already dragged them level to goals by Holden and Dawson, but it was nail-biting stuff. Preston knew the danger men to mark and were doing a good job. They did not consider Boyce a penalty box threat and certainly not with his head. But as if the fates took over it was Boyce who ghosted in and glanced the winner wide of an astonished Alan Kelly to bring the Cup back to London's East End for the first time.

Boyce was a respected play-maker before that game. He walked off a living Cockney legend whose name alone is sufficient to spark a verbal re-

CUP KINGS FOR A DAY!

West Ham's Ronnie Boyce (second left) made himself the surprise hero of the 1964 F.A. Cup Final by heading the winning goal.

run of the whole game within five miles radius of Upton Park.

Two years later, however, Boyce was utterly upstaged by a little-known Cornishman whose inclusion in the star-studded Everton side caused uproar around Goodison Park. The reason was simple, manager Harry Catterick put him in place of the idolised England striker Fred Pickering.

But Mike Trebilcock achieved football immortality as Everton staged the most exciting comeback since the Stanley Matthews Final of 1953.

Jim McCalliog and David Ford shot Sheffield Wednesday 2-0 up with nearly an hour gone. Everton looked dead until Trebilcock took over, blasting two fine goals to make it 2-2 and send the Evertonians wild. Wednesday were so shocked that the momentum of the whole situation overcame them. Derek Temple escaped to hit a late winner. But it was Trebilcock who was the toast of Merseyside.

LITTLE KNOWN

Like so many such heroes, however, Trebilcock failed to sustain his form, went to play for Portsmouth and ended up playing in Australia. Not that he minded so much. He was already a confirmed hero of F.A. Cup history.

Alan Taylor's career began in the backwaters of Rochdale where the uninspiring total of seven goals in 55 appearances nevertheless led to West Ham signing him in 1974.

Billy Jennings, Bobby Gould and Keith Robson were the recognised scorers at that time. But as Hammers swept through the F.A. Cup Rounds it was the frail, little-known Taylor who suddenly came into his own.

mis-hit a 20 yarder . . . and saw it bobble into the corner of Alex Stepney's net.

His goal sent the cream of Fleet Street diving for their match programmes in order to discover his place of birth, background and scoring record. Stokes, more than most, was a Wembley unknown. He basked in his glory but was quickly moved along the coast to Portsmouth as football's non-stop building programme made him surplus to Dell requirements.

Perhaps the oddest Wembley hero of all was Roger Osborne of Ipswich Town. The Suffolk club pulled a masterstroke against much-fancied Arsenal in 1978 by using striker David Geddis wide on their right to shut out the threat of left back Sammy Nelson.

Nelson's swift overlaps linked well with Liam Brady and served the Malcolm Macdonald-Frank Stapleton strike partnership to deadly effect. But Nelson was blotted out and it was Ipswich who steadily choked up the midfield where the unfit Brady eventually gave way to Graham Rix.

But with Pat Jennings inspired and Arsenal's tired defence looking stubborn, a score-less game seemed inevitable . . . until Willie Young miscued a right wing cross into the path of the otherwise unspectacular Osborne who promptly belted it past Jennings.

The excitement and emotion of the moment were all too much for the player who fainted and had to be replaced by Mick Lambert.

Even worse, injury in the close season meant that it was nearly two years before Osborne played for Ipswich again, but rarely can a non-playing member of a team been so widely discussed by the fans for so long.

And how ironic it was that Roger Osborne should fade quietly away from the Ipswich set-up, just as they had begun to emerge as a real force in the First Division and in Europe.

In season 1973-74 he scored only two League goals, but two goals against Arsenal in the Sixth Round and another two against Ipswich in the Semi-Final replay were enough to send Hammers back to Wembley.

It was the experienced Gould who ended up as sub . . . and Taylor who made it a hat-trick of braces with both goals to sink Fulham. Wembley was Taylor's stage that day, unlike so many shock stars he managed to sustain the limelight for another season. But the promised goal-flood did not materialise and he eventually left Upton Park.

When Manchester United's dazzling young tearaways strode out behind Tommy Docherty for the 1976 Final they were hot favourites to out-run and out-last Lawrie McMenemy's mixture of unknowns and semi-veterans.

Peter Rodrigues was a veteran of the 1969 Final between Leicester and Manchester City, Peter Osgood had done it all before with Chelsea in 1970 and McCalliog had seen the whole Wembley circus way back in 1966.

United began at 100 mph, failed to ruffle Rodrigues and Co., began to splutter and could only hang their heads when the wily McCalliog sprang their offside trap with a perfectly-timed long ball to Bobby Stokes. The little left winger scampered away hopefully,

The selection of Mike Trebilcock for the Everton Finalists in 1966 was not popular amongst their supporters. But they crowned Mike (centre) king after his two goals brought the Cup to Goodison Park.

Ipswich Town's Roger Osborne went weak at the knees and fainted after scoring the goal that captured the Cup for the Suffolk side for the first time in their history. Roger, third from left, was still in a dream at the celebrations.

Published by IPC Magazines Ltd., King's Reach Tower, Stamford Street, London, SE1 9LS, England. Sole Agents for Australia and New Zealand: Gordon & Gotch Ltd; South Africa: Central News Agency Ltd. Printed in England by Fleetway Printers, Gravesend, Kent. 85037-863-X.

TWENTY QUESTION QUIZ

Answers below right

1. Celtic beat Rangers 2–1 to clinch the 1982–83 Scottish League Cup Final at Hampden Park. Charlie Nicholas and Murdo MacLeod were on the mark for the Parkhead club . . . who scored Rangers' consolation goal?

2. (a) Kerry Dixon, (b) Dave Syrett, (c) Mark Lillis and (d) Malcolm Poskett each scored four goals in a game during last season. Which clubs were they playing for at the time?

3. Allan Simonsen (below) signed for Charlton Athletic in November, 1982. From which Spanish side did the South London club buy him for £300,000? And for which club did he appear in a losing European Cup Final in the 1970's?

4. Liverpool's Sammy Lee (right) with the European Under-21 trophy after England's 5–4 aggregate win against West Germany. (a) How did the first-leg finish and (b) was it the first time England had won the trophy?

5. England recorded their biggest win since 1965 when they thrashed Luxembourg 9–0 at Wembley in a European Championship game in December, 1982. Which striker, playing his first full game, scored a hat-trick?

6. Rearrange the jumbled letters to find the name of one of Scotland's all-time greats . . . YKNENGDHSLALI (OLLRVIOPE).

7. True or false? Keith Hackett refereed the Tottenham versus Manchester City 1981–82 F.A. Cup Final? (Spurs won 3–2 in a replay).

8. Spurs were back at Wembley the following season when they met Queens Park Rangers in the F.A. Cup Final. The first match finished 1–1, and a Glenn Hoddle penalty (below) finally gave the Cup to Spurs. Who was fouled by Tony Currie for the spot kick?